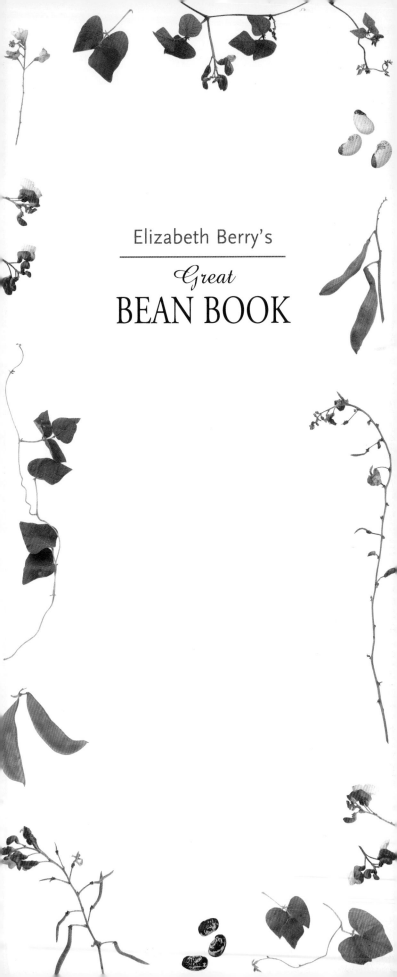

Elizabeth Berry's

Great
BEAN BOOK

Elizabeth Berry's

Great

BEAN
BOOK

Florence Fabricant

Foreword by MARK MILLER
Photography by LOIS ELLEN FRANK

Ten Speed Press
Berkeley, California

Ten Speed Press
Box 7123
Berkeley, California 94707
www.tenspeed.com

Distributed in Australia by Simon & Schuster Australia, in Canada by
Ten Speed Press Canada, in New Zealand by Southern Publishing
Group, in South Africa by Real Books, in Southeast Asia by Berkeley
Books, and in the United Kingdom and Europe by Airlift Books.

Cover and book design by Toni Tajima.

Library of Congress Cataloging-in-Publication Data
Fabricant, Florence
[Great bean book]
Elizabeth Berry's great bean book / Elizabeth Berry and
Florence Fabricant ; photography by Lois Ellen Frank.
p. cm.
Includes bibliographical references.
ISBN 1-58008-031-6
1. Cookery (Beans) 2. Beans. I. Fabricant, Florence. II. Title.
TX803.B4B47 1999
641.6'565—dc21
99-14027 CIP

Printed in Hong Kong
First printing, 1999

1 2 3 4 5 6 7 8 9 10 — 04 03 02 01 00 99

To my husband, Andrew, my children,
and my grandchildren.
—ELIZABETH

And to Richard, of course, and the
bean lovers, Patty, Robert, and Jill.
—FLORENCE

May these ancient seeds, these food sources,
always remain a part of where we came from
and who we are today.
—LOIS

Contents

ACKNOWLEDGMENTS ix

FOREWORD 1
by Mark Miller

THE HISTORY OF BEANS 7

ELIZABETH BERRY AND HER BEANS 19

BEAN BASICS 23

A GUIDE TO BEANS WITH RECIPES 28

CONTRIBUTING CHEFS 113

SOURCES FOR BEANS 115

BEANS ON THE INTERNET 116

BIBLIOGRAPHY 117

PHOTO CAPTIONS 119

INDEX 121

Acknowledgments

Many thanks to all who made this book possible.

Elizabeth Berry has special appreciation for:

Seed Savers Exchange and David Cavagnaro and Kent Whealy who generously provided so many varieties of beans; to Jose Duran, who taught her how to grow beans; to Fred Berry for his years of support and his development of the drip system; to Lawrence Standish for his artistic talent and enthusiastic encouragement; to Charles Mann for his beautiful pictures of the ranch; and to Lola Weyman for her patience in accounting for, packing, and shipping the beans.

To Mark Miller, Jeff Drew, Gary Kucy, and the staff of the Coyote Cafe; to chefs David Tanis, Katherine Kagel, Eric Di Stefano; to the chefs who contributed to this book; and to those other chefs who understand the problems of farmers throughout the years.

To Carlotta and Hugh of Wild Oats, Santa Fe, for making Gallina Canyon Ranch beans available in bulk; and to Nile, Craig, David, Herman, and Michael McLaughlin, who have also given endlessly of their time and love.

And infinite thanks to all the farmer's market customers who love our beans and support what we do.

Thanks, also from Florence Fabricant:

To Mark Miller, whose enthusiasm for what Elizabeth was doing made the fascinating acquaintance and friendship with Elizabeth possible; to Elizabeth for providing the unexpected opportunity to stretch mind and palate with the wonder of beans; to Lois Ellen Frank for her artful and tireless camerawork; and to Lorena Jones, Holly A. Taines, and Kirsty Melville of Ten Speed Press for their thoughtfully sensitive editing and support.

Foreword

I'm a bean lover and have been one all my life. Beans are one of those foods that I am emotional about, as is Elizabeth Berry. It was our passion for beans—mine for eating them and Elizabeth's for growing them—that brought us together almost fifteen years ago.

The beans of my childhood were much less exotic than the heirloom varieties Elizabeth grows on her New Mexico ranch and those we use at Coyote Cafe. My emotional attachment to beans undoubtedly began with the homey, marvelous baked beans my mom made on Saturday nights when I was growing up. Whether we enjoyed our baked beans at my grandmother's home or our own, cooking and eating them was a ritual for our New England family.

The ritual of the dinner started with sorting the small pea or navy beans on an old, stenciled black tray. The small ivory beans contrasted with the shiny black lacquer on the tray, and the gray stones were picked out—kind of like a game. The beans were then rinsed a couple of times and left to soak. The next day, they were drained and transferred to the old, cracked bean crock. A slab of glistening salt pork was added to the center, as were a yellow onion studded with cloves, a generous pinch of dried mustard, a dollop of strong molasses, a small palmful of brown sugar, and a dash of water. The crock was then sealed with the ceramic lid and spirited off to the warm oven, and we all went to sleep. During the night, the seductive aroma of the slow-cooking beans wafted through the house and into our bedrooms. No visions of sugarplums and fairies for me—my dreams were of sweet, dark beans laced with succulent threads of glazed pink ham.

I don't know whether I was so enamored with my mom's baked beans because I was teased for almost two days by the smell of them cooking or because they were really that incredible. I do know that I was always hungry with anticipation. When the bean pot was taken from the oven, some of the sauce had boiled out, glazing the crock like the finish on a piece of pottery fresh from the kiln. The bean pot was escorted from the oven to its throne on a black metal trivet on the center of the table, and the lid was gingerly removed with the heaviest pot holder. The beans had been magically transformed from dry, tasteless common pea beans to a magnificent dish. They were dark and bubbly, the salt pork rich and unctuous. The marriage of sweet and spicy, rich and earthy was simple and satisfying. Accompanied by homemade brown bread and baked ham, it was a feast. I had seconds and sometimes thirds. And when the meal was over, I longed for the leftovers and would eat the beans warm or cold. I even ate them for breakfast!

No matter how many times we had baked beans, I always looked forward to the next occasion. Even when we dined out or traveled, I would search the menu for them in my quest to find the ultimate version. I often ordered them at Howard Johnson's and Durgin Park in Boston and, although they were tasty, they never came close to the ones we had at home. Even now, after forty years of traveling and tasting the world's amazing dishes, the ritual of our Saturday night baked beans remains unrivaled in memory and taste.

For me, beans are a food with character. They have depth, and evoke (as you can tell from my digressions) a strong response. I know some people don't even like beans, but they're not invited to my house for dinner! Bean lovers are earthy and soulful, like the simpatico food they favor. Elizabeth Berry is one of these people. She is definitely one of the earthiest people I know. That's what makes her and the beans she grows so extraordinary. She's one of those rare people who faces even the most dramatic obstacles with temerity—whether it's a devastating hailstorm that ruins six months of backbreaking work in two minutes or an early frost that threatens most of the fall harvest. She accepts and even relishes every challenge. When I met Elizabeth, I could tell she was a bean person. What I didn't know then was that she had an uncanny ability for growing exotic beans.

When Elizabeth and I first began working together, the idea was for her to grow select specialty produce on her Gallina Canyon Ranch for my Coyote Cafe in Santa Fe. I had grown used to buying fine-quality produce from local growers when I was in the San Francisco Bay Area and wanted to establish the same arrangement in Santa Fe. Elizabeth offered to become a trial producer and the rest is history. The first year we grew mostly greens and salad vegetables—all varieties that had been successfully grown in California. In New Mexico, growers said it would be impossible to grow them there. Elizabeth proved them wrong the first season, and many more times over the next fifteen years.

At the end of that first growing season, we reviewed the varieties' performance and looked through the seed catalogs to plan our plantings for the following year. As we looked through the catalogs, we became fascinated by the unusual names and colored patterns of the beans available. Elizabeth contacted organizations like Seed Savers to get older, rarer, noncommercial varieties. I started to collect beans from street markets and bazaars during my travels in Mexico, Bolivia, and Peru. I also brought beans back from the markets of Spain, Italy, France, Japan, China, and Southeast Asia. Elizabeth experimented with growing them, and even from the beginning the beans grew remarkably well and the diversity was amazing. It might have had something to do with the fact that Elizabeth was farming land that was once inhabited by Pueblo Indians, for whom beans, along with corn, were an important crop. We figured the beans felt at home there.

The world of beans grew from the twenty or so that I knew to over four hundred varieties. The names were exotic: tongues of fire, painted pony, snowcap, calypso, rattlesnake, Appaloosa, Jacob's cattle, Jackson wonder. There were large beans, tiny beans, beans the size of rice, purple beans, yellow beans, pearly beans, orange beans, and intensely colored solid, mottled, and dotted orbs. Not only did they look different, they tasted different. Their creaminess, richness, earthiness, and sweetness differed. The cooking properties varied—some stayed hard, and some soaked up spices and sauces. Each year we held tastings for chefs to select the varieties for the next year's plantings.

Our guests were amazed at the plethora of beans we served. These heritage beans had a depth of flavor and richness that far outstripped the common store-bought kinds they were used to. We found the beans went with everything from buffalo ribs to lobster enchiladas; their versatility was astounding. The rest of the culinary world discovered beans, and they became fashionable again.

After being around for seven to nine thousand years, beans made a comeback in the 1980s and '90s as three-star chefs in France and America featured them on their elegant menus. The common bean was finally elevated to its rightful place in the food pantheon. Even as rare and decadent foods like truffles and foie gras became more popular and food lovers became more adventurous, beans held their own. People longed for the comfort beans promised, and even discovered their healthy properties. I don't know how many millions of research dollars were spent to confirm that obvious truth. I knew that as a kid.

Although we and our European counterparts were rediscovering beans, the rest of the world never forgot them. Beans have been an essential food in Latin America continually since their first cultivation, even though Europeans "discovered" and claimed them for themselves. (French beans are actually from the lowlands of central Mexico and the jungles of Peru, and should technically be called Latin beans.) But at least the French knew a special ingredient when they saw it, and had the good sense to create one of the world's most masterful bean dishes—cassoulet.

Looking back, I realize that beans have played an essential role in my culinary life for the last forty years. There were the baked beans I savored as a child, the luscious refried beans with queso and crema that I ate in Mexico as a young adult, the smoky and herbaceous black beans I ate three times a day for months when I was studying weaving in Guatemala, the bracing red chili with pinto beans that we cooked on the YO Ranch in Texas, and the simple black bean soup that became my first published recipe. When I started my first restaurant, Fourth Street Grill in Berkeley, California, in 1979, one of the dishes on the menu was my version of black bean soup. Within two months of opening, James Beard came to the restaurant, was delighted by the soup, and asked me for the recipe. He printed it in his nationally syndicated column, which appeared in over two hundred newspapers, forever linking my culinary career to beans.

A reliable companion to have in today's uncertain times, beans are an unassuming, honest food that make us feel as though we have eaten something "real" and that we are well fed. They are good fuel for shoveling snow on a winter night, riding across mountain ranges in the early morning, or recovering from a stressful day at the office. You can depend on them, just as you can depend on Elizabeth Berry's beans and her *Great Bean Book* to introduce you to the dizzying spectrum of colors, textures, and tastes that have captivated me and the patrons of the Coyote Cafe for so many years.

—Mark Miller
Santa Fe, January 1999

The History
of Beans

Follow the beans and you will know the story of civilization. Few foods are as closely linked to human history as beans.

Beans were an essential food for early man. The Roman term *legumen,* from which "legume" is derived, is defined as edible seeds formed in pods that can be eaten as porridge or as a purée. The noun is derived from *lego,* meaning "to gather or select."

The first more or less permanent settlements evolved when hunter-gatherers and nomads stopped roaming around and began tilling the soil. Beans or legumes, which, in this context, include all the pulses and peas, were among their original crops.

Scholars can only speculate on the origins of farming. Did some late Paleolithic individual or group discover that some seeds, set aside in the corner of a cave or in some kind of container, had begun to sprout? And that their tiny leaves looked like plants they had seen growing and whose pods they had gathered, leading to the conclusion that the seeds could be put back into the earth to grow again?

However it happened, this discovery led mankind from the rudeness of the Paleolithic era to the New Stone Age, or Neolithic period, characterized by primitive agriculture, the domestication of animals, and the crafting of tools. And beans were there.

Archaeologists have found evidence of peas in an excavation called the "Spirit Cave," on the border between what are now Myanmar and Thailand, that has been carbon-dated to 9750 B.C. The word "pea" is thought to be derived from Sanskrit. Peas subsequently became part of the diet throughout Asia and Europe.

Lentils are hardly what you'd call newcomers, but scientists have been unable to pinpoint their origins in parts of the Middle East any earlier than 6750 B.C., a good 3,000 years later, in Qalat Jarmo, in northeastern Iraq. By 5500 B.C. lentils were cultivated in western Turkey and in Anatolia. They were grown in the Hanging Gardens of Babylon. Around 800 B.C. (practically yesterday) Jacob's biblical pottage, for which he sold his birthright, is thought to have been a lentil stew.

Vestiges of fava or broad beans have been found in Neolithic excavations in Switzerland and in the ruins of Troy. Remains of chickpeas have been identified in Sicily and Persia. At least 4,000 years ago, favas, lentils, and chickpeas were buried in Egyptian tombs.

All the while, from Manchuria southward, the ancient Chinese were busy with soybeans, which were first cultivated around the Chang period, about 1500 B.C. Chinese Buddhist missionaries who arrived in Japan around the sixth century brought soybeans with them. The Japanese took as readily to the soybeans as to the religion.

At the same time, oceans and continents apart in the Americas, the haricot bean, a vast category including all the different kinds of kidney beans, lima beans, and runner beans, was becoming a staple crop, adapting to climates as diverse as the cold and damp of New England and the unrelenting desert of parts of Mexico. Evidence of bean crops dating back to 7000 B.C. has been found in parts of Mexico and Peru.

Botanically, the various kinds of beans—the lentil, the broad bean, the chickpea, the soybean and the haricot—are categorized differently. But as food, these essential, nutrient-rich plant seeds—because that's really all they are—are used almost identically.

The ancient farmers who started planting and harvesting their beans, whether in Andean highlands near Cuzco, along the Yangtze River, in the Fertile Crescent of Mesopotamia, or in the shadow of Mont Blanc, were also growing grain: corn, rice, wheat, millet, barley.

Unlike the beans, however, the various grains cannot easily be substituted one for another. Nonetheless, beans and grains perform in tandem, like Fred and Ginger. The amino acids, notably lysine and tryptophan, in beans complement those in grains to result in complete protein—one of the most essential nutrients and a building block of life and growth. How did ancient people know to grow both and eat them together? To this day, students of culinary history marvel at such instinctively sensible, nutrient-dense combinations as rice and lentils, succotash of corn and limas, and couscous with chickpeas.

In the Old Testament, the bread that Ezekiel was required to eat during a time of penitence was perfectly balanced. "Take thou also unto thee wheat, and barleys, and beans, and lentils, and millet and vetches, and make thee bread thereof" is the verse.

The North American Indians who planted the "Three Sisters," an intermingling of beans, corn, and squash in the same plot of land, were also practicing sound agriculture, cultivating three crops that were perfect complements. The beans twined on the cornstalks, which shaded them, and the squash grew between the rows, suppressing weeds. Each crop used the soil and its nutrients differently, and, when harvested together, they provided a balanced diet, one that could be stored for winter and sustain the community in times of drought.

Once the age of exploration began, and the exchange of crops between hemispheres of the Earth accelerated, from the New World to the Old World and back again, the possibilities for more grain and bean combinations increased exponentially. Mexican rice and beans, Cuban moros y cristianos, the hoppin' John of black-eyed peas and rice favored in the American South, and Venetian pasta e fagiole are some of the newer recipes in the world's repertory.

THE BIG THREE

Soybeans

Worldwide, the most important bean is the soybean. Unlike other types of beans, its use as food depends largely on its magic versatility, an ability to be transformed into something other than a mere plant seed. Instead of a plate of soybeans, millions of Asians depend on soybean sprouts, soybean curd, soybean milk, soybean noodles, soybean oil, and fermented soybean sauces like miso and soy sauce.

The Chinese and Japanese consume the most soybeans. Western travelers to the Far East, from about the thirteenth century on, all noted the soybean-based foods that were staples of the diet. But even in times of severe deprivation and famine, like during and after the Civil War in the South, or the two World Wars in Europe, Westerners did not sow their fields with soybeans, beans that are easy to plant and harvest because of their relatively brief, fifteen-week growing season. Soybeans were not cultivated on a large scale in the West until after World War II, first in the United States, then in Europe.

People consume more soybeans than any other bean on Earth. And today, the United States is the world's number one soybean producer. Vegetable protein, as in those imitation bacon bits, is made from soybeans. And unlike many kinds of beans, some strains of soybeans have a relatively high oil content. Soybean oil is a common, mostly monounsaturated cooking oil.

But as much as Americans may enjoy fake bacon on the salad bar, or prefer too much soy sauce on their "Chinese" fried rice, American soybeans are grown mainly to feed livestock, to export to China, and to use in manufacturing plastics and glue. You'll find soybean, not flageolet or cannellini, futures on commodities markets around the world.

Haricots (*Phaseolus vulgaris, Phaseolus lunatus, Phaseolus coccineus, Phaseolus acutifolius*)

The New World haricot bean gradually began taking over the plates of bean eaters worldwide, starting in the sixteenth century, when the conquistadors and other explorers began bringing them back to Europe. Christopher Columbus may have noticed them growing on Caribbean islands, but it was Cortés and his invaders of Mexico, Jacques Cartier in Quebec, and Cabeza de Vaca in Florida in 1528 who documented beans and carried them home. The name "haricot" is a corruption of the Aztec word *ayacotl.*

Within a century the haricot replaced the fava, or broad bean, as the favorite on European tables. Haricots first appealed to the Italians, especially the Tuscans, who came to be called *mangiafagioli,* or "bean eaters." (Similarly, the Papago tribe of the Sonora Desert in Arizona were called "tepary bean eaters.")

Catherine de Médicis is said to have brought haricots to France when she went there to wed Henri II in 1533. But, except in Provence, where the beans were quickly appreciated and became a luxury, the French took almost as long to acquire a taste for haricots as for potatoes, neither of which had much impact in their kitchens until the mid-eighteenth century. *Plus ça change.*

England is now the world's biggest market for canned baked beans (a dumbing down of the haricot). Heinz sells 1.5 million cans of them a day there.

That haricots were cultivated by Native Americans in a wide range of climates has led botanical archaeologists to conclude that by the time the Europeans arrived, the various Native American communities already knew which beans grew successfully in their regions and had long been practicing plant selection. Today in Mexico, about 2.5 million acres are planted with beans.

Common haricots *(Phaseolus vulgaris)* are the most varied category of beans. They grow on vines that creep along the ground or can be trained up a pole. Some are low bush plants. The family ranges from the skinny, deep green *haricot vert* of France, with microscopic seeds, which is meant to be eaten fresh, pod and all, to the giant, fat pods of runner beans containing a few enormous and colorful seeds.

Haricots range in color from white to black, with every possible shading in between. The pods in which they grow are as varied as the seeds they contain, coming in an array of tints and shapes. Some of the beans are marbleized, spotted, or otherwise beautifully patterned. They can be tiny, the size of grains of rice like the minuscule white rice beans, or they may be plump and fat. In Peru, a type of haricot called *nuñas* grows at high altitudes and is cooked by roasting because water boils too slowly. These beans burst open like popcorn and taste like peanuts.

Lima beans *(Phaseolus lunatus),* which are named for Lima, Peru, and are known to have been cultivated in coastal Peru since 6000 B.C., are thought by some scientists to have originated in Guatemala. One strain, the small-seeded lima, may have come from Mexico. They differ in shape and chemistry from haricots. Large-seeded limas are also distinct from small-seeded ones (baby limas). And all contain potentially toxic cyanogens, which are destroyed by cooking. Fresh sprouted limas are a no-no.

Runner beans *(Phaseolus coccineus)*, so-named botanically for the typical bright red (cochineal) of the plant's flowers, look something like lima beans but are invariably huge and dazzlingly colored or marbleized.

Finally, there are tepary beans *(Phaseolus acutifolius)*, many varieties of which resemble kidney beans. But they are botanically distinct because they grow in desert climates. They have long taproots. And, because of their adaptability, they are now of great interest to plant geneticists.

Fava Beans (Vicia faba)

When haricot beans from the Americas started showing up in Europe in the sixteenth century, the once predominant fava, or broad bean, a vegetable of great antiquity known to have been gathered and eaten in the Stone Age, began to lose ground. The need to peel favas' leathery skins makes it clear why the thinner-skinned haricots from the New World replaced them so easily.

Nonetheless, the taste for favas, which Americans are finally beginning to acquire, has been maintained. They were first cultivated in the Mediterranean basin—in Sicily as early as 4800 B.C., according to cave excavations, and perhaps even earlier in Egypt. A hardier, smaller-seeded strain grew in colder climates in the Caucasus. There has been evidence of fava beans in most Neolithic settlements throughout Europe, as far north as Scotland and Sweden.

The Roman family name Fabius is derived from *faba,* which evolved, in Italian, into "fava." (Curiously, another famous Roman family, that of Cicero, comes from *cicer,* or "chickpea.") In French, these beans are known as *fèves.* And the Egyptian brown beans called *ful* are a kind of small fava.

The first recorded mention of three-field crop rotation, with crops planted in two fields, allowing one to remain fallow, was in A.D.765. Fava beans—or another pulse like peas or lentils—were typically cultivated on one of the three fields, and grain was planted in the second field. Previously, the system of two-field planting was used, with each field fallow every other year. Charlemagne required that several rows of broad beans and chickpeas be grown in all gardens.

Though not as showy as haricots, favas, which come in shades from pale celadon and gold to deep purple, are among the few beans eaten fresh as well as dried. The dried beans were not only useful as storage food, they were also ground into a meal to make bread. In winter, during the Middle Ages in Europe, dried broad beans and lentils were about the only vegetables available for the masses. Beans were welcome in the diet because they could absorb the salt from the bits of preserved bacon or salted fish cooked with them. Though fava beans were eaten mostly dried, sometimes the young shoots of the plant were added to a dish to give it a fresher taste.

Some people of European descent have a genetic disorder—known in lay terms as favism—which results in a severe anemic reaction to the bean. Some are so sensitive that even the pollen of the plants can cause distress or a sudden severe respiratory problem. Pythagoras, the Greek mathematician, was perhaps the most famous victim of this malady.

BEANS IN MYTH AND MAGIC, LITERATURE AND ART

We all know of the magic bean from the Brothers Grimm. Jack, instructed to sell his mother's cow to get money for food, trades it instead for a handful of beans—magical beans. His mother tosses them out the window, and the next day the beanstalk, a spectacular route to the sky and great riches, appears.

A mere pea can test a princess. And even today, to guarantee luck and wealth in the new year, black-eyed peas are eaten in the South, and lentils go into the dish of choice in Rome.

But beans have also been the symbol of the food of the poor. In the play *Plutus* by Aristophanes, when a man has acquired wealth, he is described as "not liking lentils anymore."

Beans have symbolized the embryo, growth, and life. And since ancient times, they have been invested with supernatural powers. The Chaldeans believed the dead returned to Earth reborn as fava beans. Lentils were among the treasures buried with the pharoahs of Egypt because they were believed to help convey the soul to the heavens. Pliny the Elder recorded the belief, in ancient Rome, that the souls of the departed resided in beans. Indeed, throughout the ages, various philosophers and mystics, including the followers of Pythagoras, forbade the eating of beans as blasphemy, a desecration of the souls of one's ancestors. (His genetic intolerance of fava beans might also have been a factor.)

Even the flatulence caused by eating beans was thought by some, Plato among them, to be evidence that one had eaten a living soul!

A Greek and Roman practice for ridding a house of ghosts was to take a mouthful of beans and spit them out. Romans placated ghosts by walking through a house at midnight strewing favas behind. In Japan there is a similar rite at the beginning of the new year to banish demons.

The Greeks dedicated a temple to Kyanites, the god of beans, on the sacred road to Eleusis and held a bean festival called *Kyampsia*. The Roman version was *Fabaria*.

Many Native American nations turned to legend to explain the "Three Sisters," the practical method of planting beans, corn, and squash together. They tell of Selu Tyva, the woman whose name means "corn bean." This figure, the mythical source of these foods, brings the seeds forth from her body.

In addition to their supernatural role, beans had a practical function in ancient Greece and Rome, as tokens for the election of magistrates, with one white bean in a bowl of dark ones. When Plutarch advised, "abstain from beans," it had nothing to do with diet. He meant keep out of politics. In the Chinese game fan-tan, beans are used as counters.

According to Pliny, when the obelisk that now stands in St. Peter's Square in Rome was brought from Egypt as booty, it was buried in the hold of a ship protected by 2,880,000 Roman pounds of Egyptian lentils.

In Rome, at the time of the Saturnalia, the master of the revels was chosen by drawing beans, also the white one from a jar of dark ones. This has translated into a Christian custom for Epiphany, or Twelfth Night, when the person who receives the fava bean or, in France, the *fève,* in the cake, is crowned the king or queen of the festivities, a tradition that is still maintained with the *gâteau de fèves.*

A crock of beans, in colonial New England, set to cook slowly helped the faithful observe the Sabbath when no work could be done. Cholent, a Jewish bean dish, accomplishes the same purpose among the Orthodox today. And in Japan, the rice served at weddings is steamed with adzuki beans to tint it a festive pink color.

Before she died, Christophe de Menil, a patron of the arts who lived in Houston, hoped to commission the sculptor Richard Serra to do a monumental work in the shape of a bean.

Of a totally different dimension, but similarly inspired by the lovely shape of a bean, is the silver jewelry designed for Tiffany by Elsa Peretti. How many women today wear these beans around their necks or on their ears as tokens of some kind?

BEANS TODAY

Though beans continue to sustain the poor in many developing nations, they are acquiring a new image on the contemporary American table. We eat beans because we choose to, not because we must in order to survive. And now that the cuisines of Mexico, Peru, the Middle East, and Asia, plus the more rustic culinary traditions of France, Italy, and Spain, are tempting cooks and chefs, beans are finally being added to our typical meat-and-potatoes or meat-and-pasta diet. Like the whole grains that were first embraced during the early days of the hippie movement, beans are now appreciated by sophisticated palates in high-priced restaurants.

In addition, Americans who are aware of the importance of a balanced diet, consuming enough fiber, and reducing the amount of meat they eat are starting to acquire a taste for beans.

Still, the affluence in the United States today is reflected by a decrease in bean consumption. In the 1960s, Americans ate about $7^1/2$ pounds of beans a year, less than a cup a week. By 1984, it was down to 5 pounds per person, an all-time low.

But there are signs of change. Lately there has been a newfound interest in bean-based classics like hummus, cassoulet, cholent, and even baked beans. And the results are being felt on the farm and in food shops.

Where there were only a few kinds of dried beans sold, usually kidney beans, lentils, chickpeas, navy beans and split peas, some markets now carry more than a dozen. We can remember, not long ago, searching high and low for some dried Italian cannellini beans. Now we buy them in our supermarkets.

And as with all kinds of other foods, the interest in new, heretofore untried varieties of beans has led to a constantly increasing demand for heirlooms.

What is an heirloom? In agriculture it's a variety that has been rescued from extinction. For example, there are Department of Agriculture records showing that in 1909 there were 7,000 different kinds of apples grown in the United States. By the mid-1980s there were fewer than 1,000. Some specialized growers are trying desperately to maintain stocks of those that still exist.

It's the same with beans. And there is much more to it than merely bringing novelty and variety to the table. Instinctively, ancient populations like the Incas knew that it was important to rotate their crops to guarantee successful harvests year after year. It is often monoculture—the planting of a single crop—that causes famine, because when the crop fails there is nothing. You need biodiversity to survive.

By not putting all your eggs, or seeds, in one basket, a blight will not affect every plant, as it did during the Irish potato famine 100 years ago. Genetic variety in potato planting might have prevented that disaster.

But unlike preindustrial farming communities, modern agriculture depends on hybrids bred for high yields that require chemical fertilizers and pesticides to meet production levels. And as these crops are planted on acre after acre, they dominate the market and leave no room for less standardized but perhaps hardier varieties of yore.

Inevitably, there has been a backlash. Just as the interest in sustainability and organics has started to revolutionize the way crops are being grown. Today in Ecuador, Peru, Bolivia, and Colombia, ancient Andean crops, including beans, are regarded as natural resources. In the United States, the desire to retrieve the varieties of the past, and their flavors, inspired a grassroots movement. Small growers around the country now specialize in heirlooms. Some, like Seed Savers Exchange, develop the seed stock. Others, often small farmers like Elizabeth

Berry struggling to stay a step ahead of encroaching development, cultivate and sell the specialized harvest, finding that such crops are often more lucrative than the run-of-the-mill stuff they used to plant. Chefs delight in offering plates of heirloom tomatoes in a dazzling palette of shades and sizes. Similarly, old-fashioned beans like soldiers, scarlet runners, calypsos, and Appaloosas, that were virtually nonexistent on store shelves, are becoming increasingly available. The only problem is that their often fanciful names have not been standardized, which makes buying them occasionally confusing.

These beans are not only gorgeous to look at, with their striking patterns and colors, they also add a delectable change of pace at the table. And in appreciating them, we all profit from a better environment, better nutrition, and better tastes.

Elizabeth Berry and Her Beans

"Come on down to the ranch and see what we're doing." That invitation, casually tossed my way nearly ten years ago, was my introduction to Elizabeth Berry, who at the time was just starting her reign as Bean Queen.

I was at Mark Miller's Coyote Cafe in Santa Fe, New Mexico. Berry was in town, bringing chiles and beans from Gallina Canyon Ranch, near Abiquiu, and I thought, sure, I'll come on down. But my tenderfoot car could not manage the rutted arroyos on the track to the ranch without littering the Georgia O'Keefe landscape with my oil pan or muffler. I gave up after more than an hour and turned back.

Though less than eighty-five miles from Santa Fe, a trip to the ranch in the narrows of a red rock canyon is not for the casual visitor. It takes the best part of an hour on a horrendous dirt track up and down gullies and over scrub. Forget about it after a heavy rain. But this is where, in 1986, at the request of Mark Miller, the owner of Coyote Cafe in Santa Fe, Berry began growing some produce for the restaurant. She first planted chiles and soon branched out to beans. The beans took over.

Berry lives on the ranch she built on the Gallina River with 3,000 adobe bricks made at the ranch. She has a grand piano but no electricity. She could not understand why we did not show up. "You could have made it," she chided. It took another seven years before we finally did. That time, though we took the precaution of renting a four-wheel-drive vehicle, she fetched us in her pickup at the second gate.

In a sense it was worth the wait, because by the time we visited the ranch the bean business was going full-throttle. There is a wall of beans at Gallina Canyon

Ranch. Two, actually. Like soccer goals, a pair of ten-foot-high wire trellises face each other across a greensward. The bean plants, some 300 or so, climb straight up these trellises two by two. The foliage on each is similar, and many of the pods also look the same. Tags near the bottom identify them.

It is a living bean library yet it represents a small fraction of the thousands of kinds of beans for which seed stock exists. And my guess is that Elizabeth would like to grow them all.

Like Jack, Elizabeth got started on her beanstalks with a little more than a handful of beans, a few pounds of red-and-white ones—five varieties—that she agreed to grow experimentally for the Seed Savers Exchange. "I grew them up my cornstalks in Abiquiu," she said, "but then the deer came and ate the corn and the beans fell to the ground and got all mixed up." At a loss to know what to do, she showed them to Mark Miller, who suggested they try cooking them. "They tasted wonderful, not like ordinary beans" she said. The following year she planted others, kept track of them, and started having chefs taste them, blindfolded so they would not be seduced by their exquisite colors and patterns. One of the first winners was the calypso bean, still one of her favorites.

Berry walks along in a semi-stoop, inspecting the pods to see whether they are ready to harvest, sometimes checking the tags to verify the variety. "What have we here?" she asks, looking at a velvety green pod and picking up the tag. "Raquel. You're lovely today."

She popped a small blackish-brown bean from its pod. "This is the wild rice bean," she said. "It looks just like wild rice and has a slightly nutty flavor. They're so good." Then there are the huge white Spanish hija beans, pale purple Mexican mauve beans, and meaty chocolate runner beans among the several hundred climbing the trellis.

On the porch of the ranch house there is another library, a wall of dried beans in little jars catalogued alphabetically: Appaloosa, canellini, Christmas lima, Jacob's cattle, soldier, white Aztec. Every year a group of chefs gets to sample an assortment of beans and selects the best ones. These will go into cultivation in the spring and will be produced for sale in shops, to restaurants, and by mail.

Transforming an experimental vine or two into a commercial crop is something else again. Lola Weyman, who organizes the cultivation of Elizabeth's beans, and her growers struggle. Sometimes certain varieties never make it. It's not enough that they look pretty and taste good, they have to produce to make it worthwhile for growers.

"What goes into a bean is amazing," Berry said. "People have no idea. And the women who grow them have a real feeling for them."

Berry's timing has been masterful. She bought the ranch and started farming just when the interest in so-called Native American "lost crops" like heirloom beans began to build. A sea change in the way chefs cooked and Americans ate was also underway. No ingredient was so lowly as to be off-limits, even in fine restaurants. And even some dishes once considered too rustic for such settings, like bean salads and ragouts, were finding an appreciative audience.

And now Elizabeth's in the bean business for keeps.

Bean Basics

BUYING AND STORING BEANS

Though most people consider dried beans to be something with an indefinite shelf life, nothing could be further from the truth. The freshness of your dried beans has an enormous effect on how they cook. It's too bad beans are not sold like wine, with a vintage date.

Beans from the prior year's harvest will cook faster and be less likely to require soaking than older beans. They will also acquire a properly tender, rich texture more easily. Very old beans might never soften enough.

Connoisseurs talk of "fresh" dried beans. Fortunately, the boutique beans and heirloom varieties that come from small growers are inevitably fresh.

Beans can be stored in a plastic sack or in a canister on the pantry shelf. There is little danger that properly dried beans will sprout or become wormy.

Though you can keep beans for at least a year, it is best not to. Write the purchase date on the package and try to use any beans you buy within six months.

Canned beans are excellent to keep on hand for emergencies or to use as shortcuts in recipes for soups, salads, spreads, and stews. Store the cans upside down, to distribute any thick residue. It is usually best to rinse canned beans before using them.

COOKING BEANS

Before cooking, most recipes will advise sorting through the dried beans for pebbles or other debris. I must confess that I have all but eliminated this step because I cannot remember the last time I found a pebble. But I always rinse beans before using them.

The cooking process essentially reconstitutes the beans. They absorb water and become tender during heating. It is better to overcook beans than to undercook them.

There are three basic methods for cooking beans: The first is to place them in a bowl and cover them with cold water to a depth of 2 inches, then allow them to soak for at least 4 hours at room temperature. Drain the beans, place them in a saucepan, add fresh cold water to a depth of 2 inches, and bring them to a boil. Skim off any foam that accumulates on the surface, lower the heat to a slow simmer, partially cover the saucepan, and allow the beans to cook until tender. Depending on the type of bean, this will take anywhere from 30 minutes to 3 hours. Watch your beans from time to time as they cook and add additional water as needed to keep them well covered.

The quick-soak method calls for bringing the beans to a boil and cooking them for 2 minutes, then allowing them to soak for 1 hour. Cook them in fresh water as directed above.

Dried beans, especially those that are reliably fresh and have not been sitting on the shelf for years, can also be cooked without soaking. Indeed, many cooks do not bother with the soaking. But the beans will take up to 1 hour longer to become tender. In Mexico, for example, beans are rarely soaked. But Mexican cooking is so dependent on beans that they are also rarely old.

Cooking beans without soaking preserves more nutrients. Some kinds of beans, like lentils, flageolets, rice beans, split peas and adzuki beans, do not require soaking.

In some bean recipes, the beans are combined with other ingredients and baked for as long as 6 to 8 hours. With these recipes, which can be cooked largely untended, there's never a problem of underdone beans. But it is important to check on the beans from time to time to be sure there is enough liquid in the pot.

Another shortcut is to use a pressure cooker. Place the rinsed beans and water (3 cups of water for 1 cup of beans, plus 2 cups of water for each additional cup of beans) in the pressure cooker. Lock the lid in place. Bring to full pressure and cook for 1 minute, then remove from the heat and allow the pressure to drop. After 15 minutes, release any additional pressure. Large beans, such as runner beans, should be cooked for 2 to 3 minutes.

The one problem with using a pressure cooker is that the foam that accumulates, or debris like floating bean skins, can clog the apparatus and cause problems. Watch carefully and if anything untoward seems to be happening—strange noises, for example—bring down the pressure by placing the pot under cold running water. Some cooks say adding a little oil reduces the potential for this to happen. Whatever you do, be sure to follow the manufacturer's directions. Also, using a pressure cooker makes it difficult to gauge when the beans are done. And if you stop the cooking but find the beans are not yet tender enough, you'll have to finish the cooking conventionally, simmering the beans in a pot.

Salt and acid can toughen the skins of beans, adding to the cooking times and making some impossible to become tender at all. These ingredients should only be added at the end of the cooking period or after cooked beans have been drained and rinsed and are combined in a recipe.

BEANS AND HEALTH

When humans started eating beans, the result was a diet that was higher in protein, and another great leap for civilization. Proof of the nutritive value of beans is even recorded in the Bible. When Daniel was kidnapped with a group of children and brought to Nebuchadnezzar's court, he was offered meats and other luxurious delicacies from the king's table. But Daniel and his followers did not wish to defile themselves with the king's meat. They requested only pulses and water. Though the king was skeptical, he went along with it. And lo! After ten days they were healthier—"their countenances appeared fairer and fatter in flesh"—than the residents of the court who had eaten the king's meats.

Without beans, a vegetarian diet, like the regimens required by Jainism and Buddhism, would be impossible to maintain. Beans were also the food of the Christian fast days in Europe.

Beans are packed with more protein than any other vegetable. The amino acids in protein are essential to the growth of cells. Of the twenty-two amino acids, nine are considered essential in the diet because the body does not manufacture them. The only source for them is food. And unlike meat, which is rich in protein, beans have no fat or cholesterol.

Soybeans provide all the amino acids; other legumes contain eight, lacking only methionine. But methionine is plentiful in grains, which lack tryptophan and lysine, hence the age-old partnership.

But beans are the protein powerhouses. A single hectare (about 2.3 acres) planted with beans will yield 7.5 million calories. Planted with grain, only 4.2 million calories of food will be harvested.

Beans are also a reasonably good source of iron and of calcium. But to exploit this form of calcium the body must also consume foods rich in vitamin C, like dark, leafy greens. A number of recipes in this book include greens among the ingredients. And beans, a complex carbohydrate, are also rich in soluble fiber, known for its cholesterol-lowering capacity.

On the negative side, beans, especially lima and kidney beans, can be toxic if undercooked. And some beans, like fava beans, can cause allergic reactions.

At the World Cup soccer tournament in Paris in 1998, the doctors for the English team raised eyebrows by forbidding the players to eat baked beans during the matches because, they said, the beans, which were canned, contained too much sugar. Most nutritionists consider beans an excellent source of energy because, like most complex carbohydrates, they release it gradually, not in a rush. Could it be that the culprit was the canning recipe, not the beans? What they did say, however, was that the ban had nothing to do with the beans' potential for causing flatulence. The English went down to defeat.

THE FLATULENCE FACTOR

Since ancient times, it has been known that beans cause gas. The human digestive system lacks an enzyme necessary to break down the oligosaccharides contained in beans so they can be absorbed. Instead they pass through the intestines undigested until bacteria causes them to ferment and they are expelled in the form of gas. In some people the reaction is more severe than in others. People whose diets are high in fiber tend to suffer less from this problem.

Soaking beans, a process during which many of the oligosaccharides are leached out, is often the answer. But the soaking water must be discarded and the beans cooked in fresh water. And Beano, a commercial product that contains the necessary enzyme, seems to work. Other remedies, including cooking beans with the Mexican herb epazote, are supposed to be effective. The Mexicans should know; they rarely soak their beans. Kombu, a kind of kelp, is said to have the same effect. Ginger is frequently used as an aid in digestion. Chewing fennel seeds is another one, widely used in India. The *paan,* or handful of seeds offered as a "digestif" at the end of an Indian meal, which may include chickpeas and lentils, has a high proportion of fennel seeds.

A Guide to Beans with Recipes

ADZUKI

These small burgundy-colored beans with a snappy white stripe are of Japanese origin and are mostly used in Japanese cooking to make sweet bean desserts. They are closely related to versatile mung beans, also used in Asian cooking to sprout and to make bean threads. Their name is sometimes rendered *aduki* or *azuki*. They are also a favorite in health food circles and are easier to digest than most other beans.

But there is no need to limit these little pretties to such narrow applications. They cook relatively quickly, without soaking, and hold their shape extremely well, making them excellent for salads. Try adzuki beans instead of lentils, tossed in a vinaigrette dressing with sausage, for example. Their flavor is nuttier and not as earthy, but, texturally, they are a fine substitute.

Unsoaked, adzuki beans take about 45 minutes to cook.

Substitutes: Le Puy or beluga lentils

Adzuki and Asparagus Salad

Yield: 4 servings

The Asian origin of this bean sends the cook to Chinese and Japanese pantries. With the poached eggs, you have a lovely brunch dish or a substantial first course. Without them, it's a side dish for grilled fish or shrimp.

- 1 cup dried adzuki beans
- 3 tablespoons extra virgin olive oil
- 1 tablespoon peeled, minced fresh ginger
- 1 tablespoon minced garlic
- 1 pound medium-thin asparagus, cut on the diagonal in ³/₄-inch lengths
- 1 tablespoon soy sauce
- 2 tablespoons Asian sesame oil
- ¹/₄ cup chopped scallions
- 1¹/₂ tablespoons rice vinegar
- Salt and freshly ground black pepper
- 2 tablespoons finely chopped cilantro leaves
- 4 eggs, poached (optional)

Place the beans in a saucepan, add water to cover to a depth of 2 inches, and bring to a simmer. Cook gently until the beans are tender, about 45 minutes. Drain the beans and place them in a bowl. Fold in 1 tablespoon of the olive oil.

Heat the remaining 2 tablespoons of olive oil in a heavy skillet. Add the ginger and garlic and stir-fry briefly, then add the asparagus. Stir-fry for 3 to 5 minutes, or until the asparagus pieces are crisp-tender and still bright green. Stir in the soy sauce and sesame oil. Add the scallions and stir-fry for a few seconds, and then add the contents of the pan to the beans. Fold them together gently.

Add the vinegar, salt and pepper to taste, and the cilantro leaves, reserving a teaspoon of the cilantro if serving the beans with poached eggs.

Top each portion with a poached egg sprinkled with the remaining cilantro. With or without the eggs, the salad should be served warm or at room temperature.

APPALOOSA

In many respects, the Appaloosa, a gracefully slender, curved oval bean with mottled purple-white marking, is the classic heirloom bean. It is related to the pinto bean, a more common variety, also named for a kind of horse. Elizabeth Berry calls hers "Appaloosa," but the bean is the same as the Anasazi, named for the civilization that flourished 1,000 years ago in New Mexico, Arizona, Utah, and Colorado.

The Anasazi disappeared, leaving only their cities and settlements built into steep canyons as mute testimony to their accomplishments. And they supposedly gave us these lovely beans as well, one of many varieties now being recultivated.

Be it Anasazi or Appaloosa, the color mellows as it cooks to pink and burgundy. The bean holds its shape nicely, and delivers a richly piney, herbaceous flavor. Unsoaked, Appaloosas take about 1 1/2 hours to cook.

Substitutes: Anasazi; also Jacob's cattle, kidney, painted pony, rattlesnake

Bowl of Red with Heirloom Beans

Yield: 4 to 6 servings

When **Sheila Lukins** *wrote her* U.S.A. Cookbook, *she traveled throughout the country interviewing regional cooks and food producers. Elizabeth Berry's Gallina Canyon Ranch was on her itinerary. Her Appaloosas inspired this chili with lamb and beer. It can be made without meat, if desired.*

- 1/2 pound dried Appaloosa, Anasazi or kidney
    beans, soaked and drained
- 1 dried ancho chile
- 3 tablespoons extra virgin olive oil
- 2 red bell peppers, stemmed, seeded, and diced
- 1 large onion, coarsely chopped
- 2 pounds boneless lamb shoulder,
    cut in 1/2-inch cubes
- 2 tablespoons minced garlic
- 2 tablespoons chile powder

2 teaspoons ground cumin

2 teaspoons dried oregano

2 tablespoons unsulfured molasses

1 (28-ounce) can, chopped plum tomatoes

2 tablespoons tomato paste

1 (12-ounce) bottle lager

Salt

1 cup rice, cooked

1 cup guacamole (optional)

1/2 cup plain nonfat yogurt, stirred

1/2 cup chopped scallions

Rinse and drain the beans, place them in a saucepan, cover with cold water to a depth of 2 inches, and bring to a boil. Reduce the heat and simmer, partially covered, for about 1 hour, until tender. Drain them.

Meanwhile, soak the ancho chile in hot water for 30 minutes. Drain it, remove the stem and seeds, and purée in a blender or food processor with 2 tablespoons of the soaking liquid.

Heat the olive oil in a large, heavy pot. Add the bell peppers and onion and cook over low heat, stirring occasionally, until softened, about 10 minutes. Add the lamb, increase the heat to medium-high, and brown the meat. Reduce the heat again.

Stir in the garlic, chile powder, cumin, oregano, molasses, tomatoes and their juices, tomato paste, and beer. Add the beans and 1 or more table-spoons, to taste, of the puréed chile. Bring to a boil, reduce the heat to a simmer, and cook partially cov-ered until the meat is tender, about 1 hour and 15 minutes. Season to taste with salt and more chile purée.

Serve over rice with the guacamole, yogurt, and scallions on the side.

BABY LIMA

As distinguished from handsome big lima beans (see Christmas Lima, page 50), baby limas, possibly of Peruvian origin but probably from Mexico or Guatemala, are more delicate. Their smaller size puts them in a different botanical category than large-seeded limas. They are not as buttery, but these small, flat, off-white ovals are tender, fruity, and sweet. Imagine baby limas with sweet white corn in a light succotash. Add squash—cubed butternut, for example—and you have the "Three Sisters" that the Native Americans cultivated together: corn stalks entwined with bean vines, with squash planted between the rows.

Unsoaked baby limas take about $1^1/_2$ hours to cook.

Substitutes: none

Smoked Trout and Baby Lima Chowder

Yield: 4 servings

Here is a rich but easy soup that could do duty as a main course, served with good bread and a salad. Other seafood—shrimp, mussels, clams, or scallops—can be substituted for the trout.

$^2/_3$ cup dried baby limas, soaked, if desired, and
    drained

1 ounce slab bacon, diced

2 leeks, white part only, rinsed, trimmed, and
    finely chopped

1 pound boiling potatoes, peeled and diced

$3^1/_2$ cups low-fat milk

6 ounces skinless, boneless smoked trout

$^1/_3$ cup heavy whipping cream

Salt and freshly ground black pepper

2 tablespoons minced chives

Place the beans in a saucepan, cover them with water to a depth of 2 inches, and simmer, partially covered, about 1 hour, or until the beans are nearly tender. Skim any foam from the surface during cooking.

When the beans are done, drain and set them aside.

Cook the bacon in a heavy saucepan until it starts to render its fat. Add the leeks and continue cooking until they are tender and turn golden.

Add the potatoes and 2 cups of the milk. Simmer for about 30 minutes, or until the potatoes are tender. Coarsely mash them with a fork, leaving some chunks. Add the remaining milk and the beans and simmer for 15 minutes.

Break the trout into chunks and add it, along with the cream, to the pan. Bring to a simmer and season to taste with salt and pepper. Serve with a sprinkling of chives on each portion.

See also Dfina (pages 46–47).

BLACK BEANS

A pantry staple, black beans are often called "turtle beans." And if you want the best, look for heirloom black Valentine beans. All black beans, which are related to kidney beans, turn purplish after cooking and have a meaty texture and a rich, nutty flavor.

A number of recipe classics, including Black Bean Soup, Mexican Frijoles Negros, Brazilian Feijoada, and Cuban Moros y Cristianos, depend on black beans. Try preparing the Sherried Pinto Bean Soup on page 87 with black beans.

Unsoaked, black beans take about $1^1/_2$ hours to cook.

Substitutes: kidney

Elizabeth's Favorite
Black Turtle Bean Stew

Yield: 6 to 8 servings

This is basically a black bean chili, excellent to serve at an informal gathering.

3 cups dried black turtle or Valentine beans,
   soaked

3 tablespoons extra virgin olive oil

1 large onion, diced

4 cloves garlic, minced

1 jalapeño pepper, sliced thin

2 teaspoons ground cumin

1 teaspoon dried oregano

1 tablespoon mild chile powder, or to taste

Salt

2 tablespoons chopped cilantro leaves

Tortillas

Sour cream

Shredded Monterey Jack cheese

Rinse the beans and drain them well.

Heat the oil in a large, heavy casserole. Sauté the onion, garlic, and jalapeño until soft. Stir in the cumin, oregano, and chile powder.

Add the beans and enough water to cover the beans by 2 inches. Bring to a simmer and cook, partially covered, for about 2^1/$_2$ hours, or until the beans are tender. Be sure the beans are covered with water as they cook. Season to taste with salt.

Continue cooking for about 30 minutes more, uncovered, or until the beans have absorbed most of the water. but are still quite moist and soupy. Sprinkle with cilantro and serve with the tortillas, sour cream, and cheese on the side.

BLACK-EYED PEA

The name clearly suits this small parchment-colored rounded pea bean with its distinctive black spot. It is thought to have originated in Asia. It came to the United States via Africa, with the slaves, and has remained a favorite in African-American cookery.

Black-eyed peas have not only a very particular, unmistakable look; their flavor, slightly smoky, is also unique. They marry particularly well with pork and smoked meats like bacon and sausage, their flavor enhancing and intensifying the smokiness. They hold their shape extremely well when cooked, making them excellent for salads. The canned variety is a worthwhile shortcut.

Unsoaked, black-eyed peas take about 2 hours to cook.

Substitutes: soybeans

Hoppin' John

Black-eyed peas are as symbolic as any bean. Hoppin' John, a mixture of black-eyed peas and rice, often with sturdy greens mixed in, is a traditional good luck dish for New Year's Day. The black-eyed peas symbolize coins and the greens are dollars.

> 2 cups dried black-eyed peas, soaked, drained,
>   and rinsed
> 1/2 pound smoked ham hocks
> 1 large onion, sliced
> 1 whole hot green chile
> 2/3 cup raw white rice
> Salt and freshly ground black pepper
> 2 large bunches watercress, rinsed and heavy
>   stems removed

Place the black-eyed peas in a large, heavy saucepan. Cover them with water to a depth of 2 inches, bring to a simmer, and skim the surface. Add the ham hocks, onion, and chile. Simmer, partially covered, for about 1 hour, or until the black-eyed peas and meat are fairly tender.

There should still be about 1/2-inch of excess cooking liquid in the saucepan. If not, add more water.

Fold in the rice and season to taste with salt and pepper. Cover and simmer over very low heat for about 30 minutes, or until the cooking liquid is absorbed, the black-eyed peas and meat are tender, and the rice is cooked. Remove the pan from the heat and transfer the ham hocks to a plate.

Fold in the watercress, cover the pan, and allow to sit for about 5 minutes, to wilt the watercress. Meanwhile, remove the meat from the bones and dice it. Fold the meat back into the pan, heat briefly, and serve.

BLACK RUNNER

Though runner beans are native to Mexico, until recently they have only been cultivated in the United States for their showy flowers and have been more prized, culinarily, in England than elsewhere. The newfound appreciation of beans, however, has put runners high on the list.

Runners are beans on steroids, state fair prize–winning in size. Black runners are not as well known as their scarlet runner siblings, but for me, their flavor has the edge. These big, handsome beans, as dark and shiny as river stones, are creamy-white inside, have a uniquely sweet, elegant flavor, and hold their shape extremely well. You can use them in soups, but it would be a pity not to take advantage of their eye appeal, so select a recipe, like the following one, that is not a smooth purée. Consider marinating them, like mauves (pages 78–79).

Black runners will become tender after 1¹/₂ hours cooking.

Substitutes: scarlet runner, white runner, cannellini, chocolate, Christmas lima, Madeira, mauve, white emergo

Kale, Potato, and Sausage Soup with Black Runner Beans

Yield: 8 servings

This recipe, adapted from a Portuguese classic called Caldo Verde, *takes full advantage of the the beans' deep color to contrast bright green kale with white potatoes and ruddy sausage. It's a flexible recipe. Chard or spinach can replace the kale; other kinds of sausage, even spicy chorizo, can be used instead of kielbasa; and though Yukon Gold potatoes provide a particularly buttery texture, plain white or red-skinned potatoes are fine instead.*

> 1 cup dried black or scarlet runner beans, or
>   chocolate beans, soaked if desired
> ¹/₂ pound smoked cooked garlic sausage, such
>   as kielbasa
> ¹/₄ cup extra virgin olive oil
> 1 onion, diced

1 pound small Yukon Gold potatoes, peeled and
   sliced 1/2 inch thick
Salt and freshly ground black pepper
4 packed cups very finely shredded kale, about
   1 bunch

Place the beans in a heavy saucepan, cover them with
water to a depth of 2 inches, bring to a simmer, and
cook, partially covered, until they are tender, about 1
hour. Skim any foam from the surface during cooking.

Meanwhile, slice the sausage into rounds about 1/2
inch thick. Heat 2 tablespoons of the oil in a heavy 3- to
4-quart saucepan, add the sausage, and sauté over
medium heat until the sausage is just beginning to brown.
Remove the sausage
slices, draining well.

Add the onion to the
pan and sauté over low heat
until it is soft but not brown.
Stir in the garlic. Add the
potatoes and 6 cups of water.
Bring to a boil and simmer
for about 15 minutes,
until the potatoes are
tender. Using a slotted
spoon, transfer the
potatoes to a bowl
and, with a fork,
coarsely mash them.
Stir the potatoes
back into the cook-
ing liquid in the
saucepan. Season to
taste with salt and
pepper.

Add the kale and
sausage to the soup. Bring to
a simmer and cook just until
the kale wilts, about 8 minutes.
Remove from the heat.

When the beans are tender,
drain them and add them to the soup.
Reheat the soup and stir in the remaining olive oil. Adjust seasonings and serve.

CALYPSO

What design firm was commissioned to create the calypso bean, also called the "yin-and-yang" for its distinctive and stunning yes-and-no, hot-and-cold, white-and-black marking. Credit the creator of zebras and angelfish with a taste for edgy contrast. Calypso beans are another heirloom variety, one unique in appearance but closely related to cannellini beans.

Cooking, unfortunately, does not preserve the pattern as sharply. The beans turn mahogany and beige, a different fashion statement. But they have a delightfully nutty, slightly oniony flavor and a texture that is more crumbly than creamy. Take care to simmer them very slowly so they do not break.

Unsoaked, calypso beans cook rather quickly, in a little more than 1 hour.

Substitutes: Great Northern, cannellini, painted pony, soldier

Corn and Calypso Gratin

Yield: 6 to 8 servings

Not a succotash but a recipe that borrows from the traditional Native American combination of corn and beans, this dish takes advantage of the color contrast provided by calypsos to enhance its eye appeal. The beans also add a touch of onion flavor. Though canned or frozen corn can be used, fresh corn stripped from just-picked ears is the sweetest and best to use.

$^3/_4$ cup calypso beans, soaked if desired

1 tablespoon butter

2 tablespoons dry bread crumbs

1 tablespoon extra virgin olive oil

$^1/_2$ cup chopped onion

1 jalapeño pepper, seeded and finely minced

2 cups corn kernels

1 teaspoon ground cumin

Salt and freshly ground black pepper

2 eggs, beaten

1$^1/_2$ cups half-and-half

2 tablespoons shredded Monterey Jack cheese

Place the beans in a saucepan, cover them with water to a depth of 2 inches, and simmer, partially covered, until the beans are tender, about 50 minutes if soaked, 1 hour and 15 minutes if unsoaked. Skim any foam from the surface during cooking. Drain the beans when they are tender.

Preheat the oven to 350°. Use half of the butter to grease a 6-cup baking dish. Dust the dish with half of the bread crumbs.

Heat the oil in a skillet and sauté the onion and jalapeño until soft but not brown. Stir in the corn kernels, cooked beans, and cumin. Season to taste with salt and pepper and transfer to the baking dish.

Mix the eggs and half-and-half together and pour this mixture over the vegetables in the baking dish. Sprinkle with the cheese and remaining bread crumbs and dot with the remaining butter.

Place in the oven and bake for 40 minutes, or until set and lightly browned on top. Serve hot or at room temperature.

CANNELLINI

Along with red kidney beans and the somewhat smaller Great Northerns, the cannellini is a kitchen workhorse, a pantry staple, and perhaps the most versatile bean of all. And no wonder. Cannellini beans belong to a category known as the common bean—*Phaseolus vulgaris*—with more than 1,500 varieties. They are sometimes called white kidney beans.

In recent years, the interest in Mediterranean cooking has spurred the demand for cannellinis, which are extremely popular in Italy, especially in Tuscany. These medium-large oval white, plump, creamy-tender beans have a mild taste on their own, so they soak up the flavors with which they are cooked. Cannellinis are widely available canned, but the texture tends to be extremely soft, so they might be best suited for making a purée. In a salad, canned cannellinis must be handled with great care. It's better to simmer them from scratch.

Though the closest substitute is the red kidney bean, the color factor might make it less desirable. And Great Northerns are smaller.

Unsoaked, cannellinis take about $1\frac{1}{2}$ hours to cook.

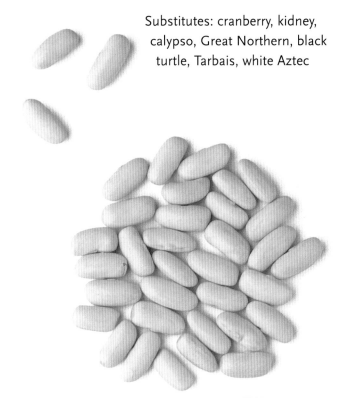

Substitutes: cranberry, kidney, calypso, Great Northern, black turtle, Tarbais, white Aztec

Warm Shrimp and Cannellini Salad

Yield: 4 servings

This dish is one of the signatures of San Domenico, a Michelin starred restaurant in Imola, in northern Italy, not far from Bologna. About ten years ago, an American branch of the restaurant, also called San Domenico, opened in Manhattan. Not only was this Warm Shrimp and Cannellini Salad, enriched with dicings of fresh tomato and perfumed with fresh rosemary, one of the restaurant's most successful and popular dishes, it was quickly copied by chefs everywhere. It has become a modern classic. And it's one of those rare restaurant dishes of such elegant simplicity that preparing it at home is not a challenge.

> 1¼ cups dried cannellini beans, soaked and
>   drained
> Salt and freshly ground black pepper
> 7 tablespoons extra virgin olive oil
> 20 jumbo shrimp, shelled and deveined
> 2 large garlic cloves, chopped
> 1 tablespoon chopped fresh rosemary leaves
> 2 medium-size ripe tomatoes, peeled, seeded,
>   and diced
> 4 small sprigs rosemary

Place the beans in a saucepan. Cover them with cold water to a depth of 2 inches, bring to a boil, lower the heat to medium, and simmer the beans, partially covered, until they are tender, about 45 minutes. Skim any foam from the surface during cooking.

Drain the beans, reserving ⅓ cup of the cooking liquid. Season the beans to taste with salt and pepper.

Heat 2 tablespoons of the oil in a large skillet, add the shrimp, and sauté, stirring, until they are golden on both sides, 2 to 3 minutes. Add the garlic, rosemary leaves, tomatoes, beans, and reserved cooking liquid. Cook, stirring gently, for 2 minutes. Again, season to taste with salt and pepper. Remove from the heat and add the remaining olive oil.

Divide the bean mixture among 4 plates, arranging 5 shrimp attractively on each. Top each portion with a sprig of rosemary and serve.

CHICKPEA

Though the lion's share of the credit, when it comes to cultivating beans, goes to the New World, especially Peru and Mexico, the Old World's chickpeas (or *garbanzos* in Spanish and *ceci* in Italy) have as impressive a pedigree. These bumpy round golden beans with a firm texture and a distinctively nutty flavor are said to have been a diet staple for more than 7,000 years. Archaeologists say chickpeas were eaten in Sicily and Switzerland during the Stone Age.

Originally grown in Asia, somewhere south of the Caucasus and north of Iran, chickpeas were cultivated in the Hanging Gardens of Babylon and are still familiar in the Middle East in hummus and falafel, among other dishes. You'll often find chickpeas in couscous.

In India, chickpeas are ground into flour and used to make pancakes and fritters, especially in the south. Throughout the world, whether in India, Africa, the Middle East, southern Italy, or Spain, where chickpeas are said to have been introduced by the Phoenicians, they sustain the poor. In the south of France, when wheat was too expensive, chickpea flour was used to make socca, a kind of crepe eaten in place of bread.

Nonetheless, in recent years, the Mediterranean diet has also put chickpeas on some pretty fancy restaurant tables in the industrialized world. For example, in New York, the chef Jean-Georges Vongerichten uses mashed chickpeas to make "fries," a kind of fritter that looks like a french fry, a clever savory that other top chefs have copied.

Chickpeas belong to the same vast family as peas, the Leguminosae, but like most of that family, technically they are not peas. And because of their firm texture, they are one of relatively few beans that are about as good from a can as simmered from scratch.

Chickpeas are best soaked, and, advises cookbook author Paula Wolfert, in soft water. "If your water is hard, I suggest you use a bottled variety; otherwise, add a teaspoonful of baking soda to the soaking water," she says in *The Cooking of the Eastern Mediterranean*. Once soaked (and rinsed in several changes of water before cooking), chickpeas require $1\frac{1}{2}$ to 2 hours to cook.

Substitutes: none

Chickpea and Feta Salad with Olives

Yield: 4 servings

Chickpeas are excellent in salads; they absorb flavors well but do not fall apart. This salad is inspired by Italy and Greece and is delicious as a side dish, on a party buffet, or on a bed of romaine lettuce as a first course.

$3/4$ cup dried chickpeas, soaked, drained, and rinsed in several changes of water (2 cups rinsed canned chickpeas may be substituted)

1 clove garlic, finely minced

4 ounces drained feta cheese, diced

12 oil-cured black olives, pitted and halved

2 tablespoons minced scallions

1 tablespoon chopped flat-leaf parsley

Juice of 2 lemons

2 teaspoons olivada (black olive paste)

$1/4$ cup fruity extra virgin olive oil

Freshly ground black pepper to taste

Place the dried chickpeas in a saucepan with cold water to cover to a depth of 2 inches. Bring to a simmer and cook, partially covered, about 2 hours, until tender. Skim the surface from time to time.

Drain the chickpeas. Place the cooked or canned rinsed chickpeas in a bowl and fold in the garlic, cheese, olives, scallions, and parsley.

In a separate bowl mix the lemon juice with the olivada and olive oil. Pour this mixture over the chickpeas and mix gently. Season with pepper and serve.

Dfina
(Moroccan Bean Stew)

Yield: 8 to 10 servings

Of North African origin, this stew is one of those slow-cooked marvels of the bean repertory. It is related to the Spanish cocida. Whether it came to Morocco from Spain or vice versa is not known. It also bears some similarity to the Jewish cholent (see page 61), and some experts believe it was popular in the mellahs, the Jewish quarters of cities in the Magreb. An Israeli dish called dafna *is also similar. This is an all-day cooking job that requires little attention once it goes into the oven.*

- 8 ounces dried chickpeas
- 8 ounces dried baby lima beans
- 3 tablespoons extra virgin olive oil
- 2 large onions, finely chopped
- 4 large cloves garlic, minced
- 2 pounds boneless lean lamb shoulder, cut into small chunks
- 1 teaspoon ground coriander
- 1 teaspoon ground cumin
- $^1/_2$ teaspoon crushed red pepper flakes
- $^1/_8$ teaspoon ground saffron
- 16 new potatoes, peeled
- 2 large carrots, peeled and cut in 2-inch chunks
- 4 eggs in their shells (optional)
- Juice of 1 lemon
- Salt and freshly ground black pepper
- 2 tablespoons toasted slivered almonds
- 2 tablespoons chopped fresh mint

Place the chickpeas and lima beans in a bowl, cover them with water to a depth of 2 inches, and soak them for at least 4 hours, or overnight. Drain well, then rinse the beans in several changes of water.

Heat the oil in a heavy casserole. Add the onions and sauté them until golden. Stir in the garlic, sauté for a minute or so, then remove these vegetables from the casserole.

Add the meat to the casserole and sauté until lightly browned. Stir in the coriander, cumin, pepper flakes, and saffron. Stir in the drained chickpeas and lima beans and the onion and garlic mixture. Tuck the potatoes, carrots, and eggs among the other ingredients. Add 6 cups of water and bring to a simmer.

Preheat oven 300°.

Skim the surface of the casserole, then cover and place it in the oven. Bake the mixture for $1^{1}/_{2}$ hours, then add the lemon juice and season to taste with salt and pepper. Place a layer of aluminum foil over the casserole and replace the lid. Bake for 6 hours longer, or until the liquid has been absorbed but the ingredients are still moist.

To serve, remove the eggs, peel them, cut them in half, and arrange them on top of the dfina. Sprinkle the dfina with toasted almonds and chopped mint.

Also see Spicy Hummus Quesadilla with Jacob's Cattle–Poblano Relish, pages 64–65.

CHOCOLATE

There's no mystery as to how these beans got their name. They are gorgeous, big, satiny dark brown runner beans with a buttery, rich flavor. Tom Phipps, a grower in Pescadero, California, developed this bean. Though you could substitute black or scarlet runners, chocolate beans have a distinctive taste. And they are magnificent on the plate, keeping their color fairly well.

Unsoaked, they take about 2 hours to cook.

Substitutes: black runner, scarlet runner, Mark, mauve, white Aztec

Chocolate Rancheros

Yield: 4 servings

This is a fairly elementary Mexican ranch-style, or "ranchero," stew adapted from a recipe used at **Mark Miller's** *Coyote Cafe in Santa Fe. What I have done is take advantage of the chocolate beans, adding a little unsweetened chocolate to the recipe, Mexican mole-style, which simply deepens the flavor. Try to find a good-quality unsweetened chocolate, one labeled either 99 percent or 100 percent chocolate. It will have better flavor and a better texture than the run-of-the-mill supermarket baking chocolate.*

1 cup dried chocolate beans, soaked

3 serrano chiles

1$^{1}/_{2}$ pounds ripe but firm plum tomatoes

3 poblano chiles

2 tablespoons extra virgin olive oil

1 onion, diced

1 ounce unsweetened chocolate, chopped

Salt

1 tablespoon chopped cilantro leaves

Rinse the beans, place them in a heavy saucepan with water to cover to a depth of 2 inches, slowly bring to a simmer, and cook slowly, partially covered, until the beans are tender, about 1$^{1}/_{2}$ hours. Be sure the beans are covered with water as they cook. When they are done, drain them.

Meanwhile, blacken the serranos in a dry cast-iron skillet or over an open flame. Blacken the tomatoes. Blacken the poblanos and place them in a plastic bag.

Seed and mince the serranos and coarsely chop the tomatoes. Peel and seed the poblanos and cut them into 1-inch strips.

Heat the oil in a large, heavy saucepan. Add the onion and serranos and sauté for about 5 minutes. Add the tomatoes and poblanos. Add 1 cup of water and the chocolate. Cook slowly, just until the chocolate has melted, then fold in the beans. Season to taste with salt. Simmer for about 10 minutes, then stir in the cilantro and serve.

CHRISTMAS LIMA

Lima, Peru, of course, is where the family known as lima beans gets its name, though some theories place its origin in Central America. Christmas limas are the largest and are among the more colorful of the large-seeded lima beans (small-seeded limas are a bit different botanically—see Baby Lima, page 32).

The quantity of limas found in archaeological digs in Peru suggests they were essential in the diet of that region. They are also depicted in fabrics and on pottery and, today, if any bean inspires artists like Elsa Peretti, the jewelry maker, it's the lima. Like cranberry beans, limas can be eaten fresh as well as dried. In the South they are appreciated as butter beans.

A popular heirloom bean, they are very large and flat, maroon with white streaks. The skin turns purple and tan as it cooks. The beans have a meaty texture and a fruity, sweet flavor.

Unsoaked, the beans take at least $1^1/_2$ hours to cook.

Substitutes: scarlet runner, chocolate, mauve

Warm Christmas Lima and Shiitake Mushroom Salad

Yield: 4 servings

Perhaps it was the almost mushroomy color of the beans once they are cooked that inspired this salad. And though the color is muted and deeper compared with the raw beans, it remains handsome on the outside with an ivory translucency within. And how better to display Christmas limas than with the red of tomatoes and green of arugula?

1 cup dried Christmas lima beans, soaked if
    desired

Salt and freshly ground black pepper

1 large bunch arugula

1 pound shiitake mushrooms, stemmed

6 tablespoons extra virgin olive oil

2 large cloves garlic, chopped

2 cups chopped plum tomatoes

1/4 cup balsamic vinegar

2 tablespoons finely torn basil leaves

Place the beans in a saucepan, cover them with water to a depth of 2 inches, bring to a simmer, and cook, partially covered, until the beans are tender, about 1 hour if soaked, about 1 1/2 hours if unsoaked. Drain the beans and season them to taste with salt and pepper. Set aside, covered, to keep them warm.

Rinse and dry the arugula and remove the heavy stems. Divide it among 4 salad plates.

Slice the mushroom caps in strips about 1/2 inch wide. Heat 5 tablespoons of the oil in a large skillet. Add the sliced mushrooms and the garlic and sauté over medium heat until the mushrooms are tender. Stir in the tomatoes.

Continue cooking for about 5 minutes, until the tomatoes have softened. Fold in the beans, the balsamic vinegar, and the basil. Again, season the mixture with salt and pepper to taste and remove from the heat.

Spoon the warm bean and mushroom mixture over the arugula and drizzle with the remaining olive oil. Serve while still warm.

CRANBERRY

Sometimes called the borlotti or Roman bean, this plump oval pinkish-brown speckled variety of common bean, like the kidney and cannellini, holds its shape well and has a mildly nutty taste. Like the cannellini, the classic cranberry made its way from South America to Europe. And now it's back.

The craze for Tuscan food has placed the cranberry second in popularity to the cannellini, but it's a bean to reckon with all the same. If anything it's a bit more flavorful than its pale cousin, and it is also the bean that is preferred in Venice.

Cranberry beans are among the few that are delicious fresh. The ecru pods are streaked with dark red, like the beans, and they are easy to shell and cook fairly quickly.

Unsoaked, dried cranberry beans take about 2 hours to cook.

Substitutes: cannellini, pinto, red or pink kidney

Pasta e Fagiole

Yield: 4 to 6 servings

Francesco Antonucci, *the chef and co-owner of Remi Restaurant in Manhattan, is a native of Venice who grew up eating Pasta e Fagiole, the classic spaghetti and bean soup. He makes a point of insisting on borlotti beans for the soup. "We don't use cannellini beans in Venice," he says. And he finishes the rustic soup with hot olive oil infused with herbs and garlic. "That trick is as old as the pyramids," he says. He also advises preparing the soup the day before it is to be served, for better flavor.*

1 $^1/_3$ cups dried borlotti, cranberry or pinto
    beans, soaked if desired

2 ounces smoky slab bacon in 1 piece

$^1/_2$ cup extra virgin olive oil

12 cloves garlic

$^1/_2$ stalk celery, coarsely chopped

1 carrot, coarsely chopped

1 small onion, coarsely chopped

1 ripe plum tomato

4 ounces dried spaghetti

Salt and freshly ground black pepper

2 sprigs each oregano, rosemary, and thyme

If the beans have been soaked, drain them. Heat the bacon and 2 tablespoons of the oil in a heavy 4- to 5-quart saucepan. Add half the garlic, unpeeled, and the celery, carrot, onion, and tomato. Cook for a few seconds, then add the beans and 5 cups of cold water. Bring to a simmer and cook, partially covered, for about 1 to 2 hours, or until the beans are tender. Skim the surface if necessary.

While the beans are cooking, bring a pot of water to a boil for the spaghetti. Wrap the spaghetti in a cloth towel or napkin and, holding the ends of the cloth closed, run this "package" of spaghetti over the edge of a counter to break the raw spaghetti into small pieces. Drop the spaghetti into the pot of boiling water and cook it for about 8 minutes, then drain it and set it aside.

When the beans are tender, remove the bacon and the garlic cloves and, using a slotted spoon, remove about half of the beans. Purée the remaining bean soup mixture in a blender or a food processor. Add up to 1 cup of water if the mixture is too thick.

Transfer the puréed soup to a saucepan. Add the cooked spaghetti and reserved beans. Reheat and season to taste with salt and pepper.

Just before serving, peel and crush the remaining garlic. Heat the remaining olive oil in a skillet and add the peeled garlic and the sprigs of oregano, rosemary, and thyme. Cook for 5 minutes, then strain the hot herb oil into the soup. Serve immediately.

Fresh Shell Bean Gratin

Yield: 4 to 6 servings

Alice Waters, *the chef and owner of Chez Panisse in Berkeley, California, and one of the most influential figures in American cooking in the past quarter century, has long been a fan and supporter of Elizabeth's work with heirloom vegetables, not just beans. One of Alice's favorite bean dishes calls for fresh, not dried, "shell" beans: cranberry, fava, flageolet, and such. If you find them in the market in summer or early fall, buy some and prepare this lovely dish. Though it can also be made with dried beans, it is better with the fresh ones.*

> 2 to 3 pounds fresh shell beans, such as
>   cranberry beans, unshelled
> Salt
> 6 tablespoons extra virgin olive oil
> $^1/_2$ onion, diced
> 4 cloves garlic, slivered
> 1 or 2 sage leaves, chopped
> 1 cup coarsely chopped rinsed Swiss chard
> 2 ripe tomatoes, coarsely chopped
> Freshly ground black pepper
> $^1/_2$ cup toasted bread crumbs

Shell the beans. You should have about 2$^1/_2$ cups. Place them in a saucepan, cover them with water to a depth of 1 inch, and bring to a boil. Add salt to taste and 2 tablespoons of olive oil, reduce the heat to a simmer, and cook the beans until they are tender, about 30 minutes. Drain the beans, reserving the liquid.

Meanwhile, heat 2 tablespoons of the oil in a large, heavy skillet. Add the onion, garlic, and sage. Season with salt. Cook over low heat until soft and translucent. Add the chard and the tomatoes and cook for another minute or two. Remove from the heat.

Preheat the oven to 350°.

Lightly oil a shallow 4-cup gratin dish. Fold the beans into the onion mixture, season to taste with salt and pepper, and spread into the gratin dish. Add enough reserved bean water to barely cover the ingredients. Drizzle with the remaining oil and dust the top with the bread crumbs. Bake for 45 minutes, adding a little more of the liquid during baking if the gratin seems too dry.

FAVA

Given a choice, I'd eat fava beans fresh, not dried. Either way, these fairly large beans are a chore. Not only must the fresh ones be shelled but both then require that their leathery outer skins be peeled either before or after cooking. Only the tiniest, most tender fresh ones can be palatable unpeeled.

The first fresh, verdantly pea-green favas are eaten raw, as a snack, with pecorino or Basque sheep's milk cheese in Italy and France.

Like chickpeas and lentils, fava beans, also called "broad beans," are an Old World variety. Not only that, they have the distinction of being the only beans that might be of European origin. They can withstand colder climates than other beans can. In France they are called *fèves* and, dried, are hidden in a traditional cake for Epiphany, the feast of the Three Kings.

Favism, an anemic allergic reaction to fava beans, occurs in some people of Mediterranean descent.

Dried favas are large, flat, pale green, purple, or yellow, with an herbaceous, chestnut flavor and floury texture.

Favas must be soaked, then peeled. Cooking takes 1^1/$_2$ hours.

Substitutes: none

Fava Bean Dip

Yield: 6 servings

Bean purées of all kinds make excellent cocktail dips. Use favas for this uniquely herbaceous one.

1 1/2 cups dried fava beans

4 garlic cloves

2 scallions, coarsely chopped

2 tablespoons coarsely chopped cilantro

2 tablespoons coarsely chopped fresh mint

1/3 cup extra virgin olive oil

1 1/2 teaspoons ground cumin

1 1/2 teaspoons hot paprika

1/4 cup freshly squeezed lemon juice

Salt and freshly ground black pepper

Toasted pita, cut into thin wedges

Place the fava beans in a bowl, cover them with water to a depth of 2 inches, and allow them to soak overnight. The next day, drain the beans and peel off the skins. Place the beans in a saucepan, cover them with cold water to a depth of 2 inches, and simmer, partially covered, until the beans are very tender, about 1 1/2 hours. Drain.

Turn on a food processor. With the machine running, drop in the garlic, scallions, cilantro, and mint and process until finely minced. Remove 2 tablespoons of this mixture and set aside.

Add the beans, 1/4 cup of the olive oil, the cumin, paprika, and lemon juice to the food processor and process until smooth. Season to taste with salt and pepper.

Place the purée in a shallow dish and drizzle with the remaining olive oil. Sprinkle the reserved herb and garlic mixture on top and serve with pita bread for dipping.

FLAGEOLET

As much as I am impressed with some of the fabulously patterned heirloom beans like Appaloosas and Christmas limas, I confess a delight in flageolets. These small celadon ovals with a delicately herbaceous taste and buttery texture soak up flavors and richly enhance all sorts of dishes. They are a French classic with roast or braised lamb. And because they hold their shape extremely well, they are splendid in salads.

Flageolets—even the name is French—are actually an early harvest of immature white beans, or haricots.

Flageolets need no soaking and cook in 45 minutes to 1 hour.

Substitutes: none

Braised Flageolets with Smoked Bacon and Wilted Kale

Yield: 6 servings

*Chef **Bradley Ogden,** who owns the Lark Creek Inn in Larkspur, north of San Francisco, has long been a fan of Elizabeth's beans. Here is his rather unusual recipe for delicate flageolets, soaking them first, then blanching them before cooking them with rich, savory, slightly smoky seasonings. The preparation guarantees they will be tender. He recommends serving them with grilled sausage or meaty grilled fish.*

1 cup dried flageolets, soaked

Salt

2 ounces smoked bacon, cut in 1-inch pieces

2 stalks celery, sliced thin

2 small carrots, peeled and cut on the diagonal
in 1-inch pieces

$^1/_2$ onion, chopped

8 cloves garlic, minced

$^1/_4$ cup seeded, minced poblano chile

1 small red bell pepper, roasted, seeded and
diced

2 cups chicken stock

1 cup balsamic vinegar

1 tablespoon red wine vinegar

1 cup diced tomato

6 ounces kale, rinsed, stemmed, and coarsely
chopped

$^1/_4$ teaspoon dried red chile flakes, or to taste

Freshly ground black pepper

Drain the beans and place them in a heavy saucepan.
Cover them with salted cold water and bring to a boil.
Drain and rinse the beans in cold water.

Place the bacon in the saucepan and cook over
medium-high heat until the fat has rendered and the
bacon is lightly browned. Remove the bacon from the
pan. Add the celery, carrots, onion, garlic, chile, bell pepper, and beans. and sauté for 5 minutes.

Add 1 cup of water, the stock, balsamic and red
wine vinegars, and tomato. Bring to a simmer,
reduce the heat, cover, and
cook very slowly for
about 40 minutes, or
until the beans are ten-
der. Season to taste
with the salt,
chile flakes,
and pepper.
Fold in the
bacon and kale,
cook just long
enough to wilt the
kale, then serve.

GREAT NORTHERN

If the kidney bean is the staple of the American South-west, the Great Northern, as in the northern part of the Midwest, is the all-purpose bean for the rest of the country. It's probably the most widely used and readily available dried bean of all in the United States.

The name is commercial but has acquired the generic meaning, like Kleenex. It's a common bean, in the same family as Italy's cannellini and the kidney bean, that probably originated in Peru or in Mexico. And it's widely available, unlike the fabulously patterned heirloom beans of the same family.

A medium-small white oval bean, the Great Northern has a slightly nutty taste and mealy texture, making it better for baking or soup-making than for salads.

Unsoaked, Great Northerns take about 1 hour and 15 minutes to cook.

Substitutes: cannellini, cranberry, navy, pinto, red or pink kidney

Cholent with Pastrami

Yield: 8 servings

Cholent is Jewish Sabbath food, a dish that is traditionally set into the oven to cook, untended, during the day of rest. It is ready to eat at sundown. Using pastrami gives it a slightly spicy flavor.

1 pound dried Great Northern beans

$^1/_4$ cup chicken fat or vegetable oil

2 large onions, chopped

3 shallots, chopped

3 cloves garlic, chopped

1 broiling chicken, cut into 8 pieces

2 pounds boneless flanken or brisket, cut into
2-inch chunks

8 ounces pastrami, in 1 piece

1 tablespoon sweet Hungarian paprika

1 tablespoon honey

$^1/_2$ cup pearl barley

Salt and freshly ground black pepper

Place the beans in a bowl, cover them with cold water to a depth of 2 inches, and allow them to soak for at least 5 hours, or overnight.

Heat the fat or oil in a large, heavy casserole, at least 7-quart capacity. Add the onions and shallots and sauté until golden. Stir in the garlic. Remove these vegetables from the pan, draining them well, and set aside.

Brown the chicken pieces in the fat and then remove them. Brown the chunks of beef in the fat and then remove them. Cut the pastrami into 1-inch squares and stir them in the fat. Then stir in the paprika and the honey. Return the onions, shallots, garlic, chicken, and beef to the casserole. Stir in the barley. Drain the beans and add them to the casserole.

Preheat the oven to 400°.

Add 6 cups of boiling water to the casserole. Cover and place it in the oven. Bake for 30 minutes.

Reduce the heat to 250° and bake for 30 minutes longer. Remove the lid, season to taste with salt and pepper, then cover the casserole with a piece of aluminum foil and replace the lid. Place it in the oven and bake for 7 to 8 hours or overnight.

HIJA

In Greece, where these beans are aptly called *gigandes,* they are cooked until tender and served, bathed in olive oil, garlic, and fresh oregano, as part of the meze, or assorted appetizers. Recently, they have become available in the United States, and Elizabeth Berry has also cultivated them, calling them "hija beans." This is one of her most successful varieties, yielding nearly 5,000 pounds a year.

Hija beans are huge, white, and slightly flattened, with a bland, somewhat sugary flavor and a toothsome, if rather dry texture. They break easily, which is why they are excellent in soup or well-anointed with olive oil.

Hija beans should be soaked prior to cooking, otherwise they may take more than 2 hours to cook and will be more prone to breaking.

Substitute: large white lima, white emergo

Turkish Bean Soup with Lemon

Yield: 4 servings

I first had this soup more than thirty years ago in a tiny neighborhood restaurant in Istanbul. Long before I knew what gigandes were, I was impressed with the size of the pieces of bean that were mingled with the purée in this delicious soup. For years I prepared it with large lima beans. But now, with gigandes, or Elizabeth's hijas, the recipe is better than ever.

1 tablespoon extra virgin olive oil

$^1/_2$ cup finely chopped onion

1 cup hija or gigande beans, soaked and drained

Approximately 1 quart well-flavored chicken stock

Salt and freshly ground black pepper

1 tablespoon freshly squeezed lemon juice

1 tablespoon plain yogurt

1 lemon cut into 4 wedges

4 sprigs oregano

Heat the olive oil in a large saucepan. Add the onion and sauté until soft but not brown. Add the beans and stock, bring to a simmer, and cook, covered, for about 2 hours, or until the beans are tender. Add additional stock if necessary.

Remove the beans with a slotted spoon and coarsely mash them. There should still be some pieces of bean.

Return the mashed beans to the saucepan. Season to taste with salt and pepper. Add the lemon juice and bring to a simmer. Remove the soup from heat and stir in the yogurt.

Serve immediately, garnishing each serving with a wedge of lemon and a sprig of oregano.

JACOB'S CATTLE

Cowhide. That's what these beans resemble. That they may also be called dalmatians, as in the spotted dog, is relatively easy to understand, though Jacob's cattle seems to me both more appropriate and more romantic, what with the biblical over-tones. (Never mind that these beans originated in Mexico, not Mesopotamia.)

Jacob's cattle beans are a tepary bean, suited to desert climates. These beans have a relatively short grow-ing season, so they have also been able to flourish in New England since Bible-toting Colonial times, making them an heirloom that never went out of style. They are truly lovely, cooking to a velvety texture with a nutty flavor.

Soaking is not essential; unsoaked, Jacob's cattle beans take about 1 1/2 hours to cook.

Substitutes: Appaloosa, Mayflower, painted pony, Raquel, rattlesnake, Swedish brown, Steuben yellow eye

Spicy Hummus Quesadilla with Jacob's Cattle–Poblano Relish

Yield: 4 servings

Bobby Flay, *the chef and co-owner of Mesa Grill in Manhat-tan, has married the Middle East and Mexico in this recipe for quesadillas filled with hummus and served with a spicy bean relish. The relish can even be served warm, as a vegetable.*

6 cloves garlic

3/4 cup chickpeas, soaked, or 2 cups canned chickpeas, drained and rinsed

3/4 cup Jacob's cattle beans, soaked

3 tablespoons freshly squeezed lemon juice

2 tablespoons tahini

1/2 cup extra virgin olive oil, preferably California

Salt and freshly ground black pepper

2 tablespoons finely chopped cilantro leaves

1 poblano chile, roasted, peeled, and finely chopped

2 tablespoons finely chopped fresh thyme

12 (6-inch) flour tortillas

1 cup grated Monterey Jack cheese

1 cup grated white Cheddar cheese

1 cup julienned zucchini

$1/2$ cup crumbled goat cheese

$1/4$ cup chile powder

Preheat the oven to 350°. Wrap the garlic in aluminum foil, place it in the oven, and roast it for 1 hour. Remove, allow to cool, and peel.

Meanwhile, drain the chickpeas and Jacob's cattle beans. Place each in a separate saucepan, cover with cold water to a depth of 2 inches, bring to a simmer, and cook, partially covered, for about 1 hour, until the beans are tender.

Place the cooked chickpeas, garlic, 1 tablespoon of the lemon juice, and the tahini in the bowl of a food processor and process until smooth. Slowly add 2 tablespoons of the olive oil through the feed tube. Season to taste with salt and pepper. Fold in the cilantro and set aside. This is the relish.

When the Jacob's cattle beans are cooked, drain and mix them with the poblano chile, the remaining lemon juice, 4 tablespoons of the olive oil and the thyme. Season to taste with salt and pepper and set aside.

Preheat the oven to 450°.

Place eight of the tortillas on an ungreased baking sheet. Spread $1/4$ cup of the chickpea mixture on each. Top each with 2 tablespoons of the Monterey Jack, 2 tablespoons of Cheddar, 2 tablespoons of zucchini, and 1 tablespoon of goat cheese. Season with salt and pepper.

Stack the tortillas to make four 2-layer tortillas and top each with 1 of the remaining tortillas. Brush the tops with olive oil and sprinkle with chile powder.

Place in the oven and bake for about 10 minutes, or until the tortillas are slightly crisp and the cheese has melted. Cut each into quarters and serve topped with the Jacob's cattle bean relish.

KIDNEY

Perhaps the most common of the common beans, the classic kidney-shaped curved oval, medium-size, meaty bean actually comes in shades of pink to red to mahogany. Kidney beans are widely available canned and these days are often packed according to color. And though the canned beans are relatively reliable and less fragile than their white cannellini cousins, they do not deliver the slightly smoky flavor that kidney beans often have when cooked from scratch. It pays to bear that in mind, when deciding how to prepare a recipe.

Unsoaked, kidney beans take about $1^1/2$ hours to cook.

Substitutes: cranberry, cannellini, pinto

Penne with Kidney Bean Ragù

Yield: 4 servings

In the United States, pasta dishes are rarely made with beans. But in Italy, pasta with beans is not uncommon. And it's not just in the Venetian soup Pasta e Fagiole (see pages 53–54). Spaghetti with chickpeas is an old Neapolitan dish. Like rice and beans, corn and beans, and other grains and beans, the combination provides complete protein. Beans, in this context, are a poor man's meat. Here is a lusty pasta dish made with beans and meat. But the beans make it possible to stretch a small ration of ground beef to provide four ample servings.

$^1/2$ cup dried kidney beans, soaked if desired,
and drained (or $1^1/2$ cups canned kidney
beans, rinsed)

3 tablespoons extra virgin olive oil

1 large onion, finely chopped

4 large cloves garlic, minced

$^1/2$ teaspoon fennel seeds

$^1/2$ teaspoon crushed black peppercorns

1 teaspoon dried oregano

1/2 pound ground beef

1/2 cup dry red wine

2 cups finely chopped ripe tomatoes or canned
plum tomatoes

Salt and freshly ground black pepper

1 pound dried penne

2 tablespoons chopped flat-leaf parsley

Freshly grated Italian Parmesan cheese

If using dried beans, place them in a saucepan, cover with water to a depth of 2 inches, bring to a simmer, and cook, partly covered, about 1 1/2 hours. Drain.

While the beans are cooking, heat the oil in a heavy saucepan. Add the onion and garlic and cook over low heat until they are very soft but not brown. Stir in the fennel seeds, peppercorns, oregano, and ground beef and cook, stirring, until the beef has lost its color and is broken into fine bits. Increase the heat to medium and continue cooking for another 10 minutes or so, or until the beef and onions start to brown. Stir in the wine.

Cook for a few minutes longer, until most of the wine has evaporated. Add the tomatoes, cover, and cook over medium heat for about 30 minutes. Season to taste with salt and pepper.

When the beans are nearly tender, bring a large pot of salted water to a boil for the penne. Add the penne to the pot and cook for 10 to 12 minutes, or until the pasta is al dente.

Meanwhile, drain the beans and fold them into the meat sauce. Bring to a slow simmer.

Drain the penne and add it to the pot with the sauce. Heat briefly, season to taste with salt and pepper, fold in the parsley, and serve with the Parmesan cheese on the side.

See also Mixed Baked Beans (pages 82–83).

LENTIL

Lentils are among the most ancient of all legumes. They were first cultivated in the Middle East around the time that wheat and barley were first domesticated, as is evidenced by carbonized vestiges dated back to Neolithic times, around 7000 B.C. With the advance of agriculture throughout the Middle East and Europe came lentils. They were found in Egyptian tombs, to nourish the pharaohs on their voyages to the afterlife. In the Bible, the "mess of pottage" for which Jacob sold his birthright to Esau in the Book of Genesis was none other than a bowl of cooked lentils.

A versatile crop, lentils are grown in Turkey and India, in parts of Europe, especially central France, in the United States, and in Canada. American and European lentils are usually brownish, greenish, or black and are sold whole. In India, the world's largest market for lentils, red lentils *(masoor dal)* are split and peeled, cook in a twinkling, and are not as earthy-tasting as whole lentils. Split red lentils are often used as a thickener in soups and sauces in India. Lentils are second only to soybeans in the amount of protein they provide.

Lentils were a popular staple food in France until the seventeenth century, when they began to be viewed as fit only for the poor or as horse fodder. The deprivation of the French Revolution and the Continental blockade put them back on the table. Recently, the tiny, round French Le Puy lentils have become very stylish, and they're especially good in salads.

Lentils do not need soaking and cook in 20 to 30 minutes.

Substitutes: If necessary, you can substitute one kind of lentil for another, but that's about as far as it goes.

Lentil Salad with Lemon Vinaigrette

Yield: 4 to 6 servings

*For **Alfred Portale** of the Gotham Bar & Grill in Manhattan, a chef who trained in France, having French Le Puy lentils has been a particular delight. He takes advantage of their excellent integrity in this sprightly salad. Though most lentil recipes do not require soaking, he feels the brief cold water bath improves their texture.*

1 pound dried French green Le Puy lentils

2 cups chicken stock

1 small onion, peeled and halved

4 small garlic cloves, peeled and crushed

1 carrot, peeled and finely chopped

1 rib celery, finely chopped

$^1/_2$ cup cornichons (small French vinegar pickles), finely chopped

$^1/_4$ cup finely chopped shallots

$1^1/_2$ tablespoons freshly squeezed lemon juice

3 tablespoons red wine vinegar

1 teaspoon Dijon mustard

$^3/_4$ cup peanut or grape-seed oil

Coarse salt

Freshly ground white pepper to taste

2 tablespoons finely chopped flat-leaf parsley

Place the lentils in a large bowl, cover them with cold water to a depth of 2 inches, and allow to soak for 30 minutes. Drain.

Place the lentils in a large saucepan, add 6 cups of cold water, the stock, onion, and garlic. Bring to a boil, reduce the heat to low, and simmer until just tender, about 30 minutes. Drain the lentils, discarding the onion and garlic. Transfer the lentils to a large bowl. Fold in the carrots, celery, cornichons, and shallots.

In a medium bowl, whisk the lemon juice, vinegar, and mustard together. Slowly whisk in the oil. Season to taste with salt and white pepper. Pour this dressing over the lentils, toss gently to mix, adjust seasonings, and allow to stand for 1 hour before serving. Fold in the parsley and serve.

Lentil Soup with Duck Sausage and Sherry

Yield: 4 servings

It's easier to purée regular brown lentils than the French Le Puy variety. Red lentils can also be used.

1 tablespoon unsalted butter

$^1/_2$ cup finely chopped onion

1 leek, trimmed, well rinsed, and chopped

2 cloves garlic, minced

1 teaspoon ground cumin

1 cup brown lentils

Approximately 5 cups well-flavored chicken
    stock

8 ounces duck sausage

Salt and freshly ground black pepper

$^1/_2$ cup medium-dry sherry

1 tablespoon minced fresh chervil

Heat the butter in a heavy 3-quart saucepan. Add the onion, leek, and garlic and cook over medium heat until the vegetables are golden. Stir in the cumin.

Add the lentils and the chicken stock, bring to a simmer, and cook, partially covered, until the lentils are tender, about 45 minutes.

While the lentils are cooking, grill or sauté the duck sausage until it is browned and cooked through. Set it aside.

Purée the lentils in a food processor, then add the purée to the saucepan. Bring to a simmer and season to taste with salt and pepper. Stir in the sherry. Slice the duck sausage in thin rounds and add it to the soup. Adjust seasonings and, if necessary, thin the soup with a little more stock. Serve with a sprinkling of chervil.

Curried Red Lentil and Grilled Chicken Casserole

Yield: 6 servings

Substitute any lentils for the red ones in this recipe, a lusty curry.

3 tablespoons extra virgin olive oil or peanut oil

1 cup finely chopped onion

1 red bell pepper, cored, seeded, and chopped

1 fresh jalapeño pepper, seeded and minced

2 cloves garlic, minced

1 teaspoon peeled, minced fresh ginger

2 teaspoons ground cumin

1 teaspoon ground turmeric

1 teaspoon ground coriander

2 skinless and boneless chicken breasts,
   coarsely diced

4 cups well-flavored chicken stock

2 cups dried red lentils

Salt and freshly ground black pepper

$1^{1}/_{2}$ cups raw basmati rice

1 cup plain yogurt

1 tablespoon minced fresh mint

Preheat the oven to 375°.

Heat the oil in a large, heavy ovenproof casserole. Add the onion, bell pepper, jalapeño, garlic, and ginger and sauté until lightly browned. Stir in the cumin, turmeric, and coriander. Add the chicken to the casserole and cook it briefly, stirring the pieces to sear them.

Add the stock and lentils. Bring to a simmer and season with salt and pepper.

Cover the casserole and place it in the oven. Cook for about 40 minutes, or until the lentils are tender.

While the casserole is baking, rinse the rice in cold running water, drain it, and place in a saucepan with $2^{1}/_{3}$ cups of water. Bring to a boil, reduce the heat to a slow simmer, cover, and cook for about 15 minutes, or until the rice is tender. Set the rice aside in the saucepan, still covered.

Mix the yogurt with the mint. Serve the casserole with the rice and yogurt sauce on the side.

Calamari and Beluga Lentil Risotto

Yield: 4 servings

Shiny black beluga lentils from the Middle East look exactly like grains of caviar. They turn brownish when cooked and, in this recipe, their inky cooking liquid is used to simmer a risotto with squid, an adaptation that definitely borrows from the classic squid-ink risotto of Venice. It's a delectable and unusual dish, worthy of a festive occasion. If beluga lentils are not available, French Le Puy lentils can be used, but the rice will not be as dark.

1 cup black beluga lentils or French Le Puy
   lentils

12 ounces cleaned squid

3 tablespoons extra virgin olive oil

1 onion, finely chopped

2 cloves garlic, minced

$1/2$ teaspoon crushed red pepper flakes, or to
   taste

$3/4$ cup arborio rice

$1/2$ cup dry white wine

$1/2$ cup fish stock

Salt

1 tablespoon finely minced flat-leaf parsley

Place the lentils in a saucepan, add 5 cups of cold water, bring to a simmer, and cook, skimming the surface from time to time, until the lentils are tender, about 25 minutes.

While the lentils are cooking, slice the squid into very thin rings.

In a heavy, nonstick 3-quart saucepan, heat 1 tablespoon of the oil until it is very hot. Add the squid and cook, stirring, for about 1 minute, until it turns opaque. Transfer the squid and any cooking liquid to a small mixing bowl.

Add another tablespoon of the oil to the saucepan. Add the onion and garlic and sauté over medium-low heat until they are tender. Stir in about half of the red pepper. Stir in the rice and cook for a few minutes. Stir in the wine. Cook, stirring, until the wine has nearly evaporated. Stir in the fish stock and cook, stirring, until it has nearly evaporated. Remove the pan from the heat.

By this time the lentils should be tender. Drain them through a strainer, catching the cooking liquid in a bowl. Return the lentils to the saucepan in which they were cooked, fold in the remaining olive oil, and season to taste with salt and the remaining crushed red pepper. Set aside.

Reheat the saucepan with the rice. Add $2^1/_2$ to 3 cups of the lentil cooking liquid $^1/_2$ cup at a time, stirring continuously, adding additional liquid as each $^1/_2$ cup is absorbed by the rice. When you have added $2^1/_2$ cups or so, the rice should be nearly tender. Add another few tablespoons of the liquid and fold in the lentils, squid, and any liquid from the squid. Adjust seasonings, fold in the parsley, and serve.

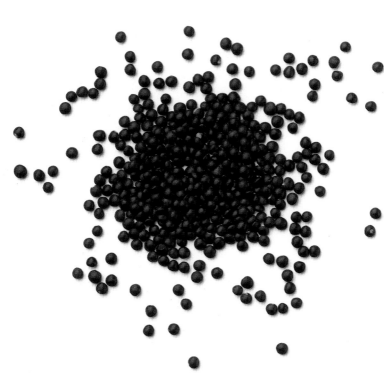

MADEIRA

Big, mottled-brown, flat ovals that are the largest of the cranberry bean family, Madeiras are so named because these common beans, found in South America, were brought back to Portugal. Then, to complete the circle in one of those "goes-around-comes-around" routines, the Portuguese carried them to the New World again. Madeiras are relatively rare; Elizabeth has slightly more than 200 pounds a year to sell.

Madeiras have a floury texture and distinctly chest-nutty flavor. I love them cooked and simply sautéed with a heap of caramelized onions. They are positively delicious tossed in with Venetian liver and onions.

Beans this size are best when soaked; unsoaked, Madeiras take at least 1 1/2 hours to cook.

Substitutes: cranberry, mauve, scarlet runner

Madeira Beans with Salt Cod

Yield: 4 to 6 servings

This dish takes its inspiration from the Iberian Peninsula. Salt cod, so typical of the cooking of Spain and Portugal, is combined with the beans in a one-dish main course. And as long as you have to soak the fish, you might as well soak the beans, too.

1 pound boneless dried salt cod

1 pound dried Madeira beans, chickpeas, or
   large white beans like white Aztecs

3 large onions

1 carrot, peeled

1 leek

2 bay leaves

1/3 cup flour

1 1/2 cups extra virgin olive oil

4 large cloves garlic, finely chopped

1 cup tomato purée

Salt and freshly ground black pepper

1 tablespoon chopped flat-leaf parsley

Cover the salt cod with cold water and allow it to soak in the refrigerator for 24 hours or longer, changing the water at least 3 times during the soaking, until the fish is sufficiently desalinated. Test it by tasting.

At the same time, cover the beans with cold water to a depth of 2 inches and soak overnight. Drain and transfer the beans to a casserole.

Add fresh cold water to a depth of 2 inches, along with 1 of the onions, the carrot, the leek, and 1 bay leaf. Bring to a boil, skim any foam from the surface, then simmer slowly, partially covered, until the beans are tender, about 1 hour and 15 minutes. Drain the beans, reserving 2 cups of the cooking liquid. Discard the vegetables. Rinse and dry the casserole and set it on the stove.

While the beans are cooking, drain the salt cod, dry it, and cut it into 2-inch cubes. Dust with flour. Heat the oil in a wok or skillet and quickly brown the pieces of cod. Drain on paper towels. Skim 3 tablespoons of the oil from the wok or skillet into the casserole and place over low heat.

Slice the remaining onions very thin. Slowly sauté the onions in the casserole until lightly browned, about 15 minutes. Remove half of the onions from the casserole, then add the garlic and sauté for a few minutes. Add the tomato purée and the remaining bay leaf and cook for 15 minutes longer.

Return the beans to the casserole along with the reserved cooking broth. Cook over medium heat for 5 to 10 minutes, or until the tomato liquid begins to thicken. Season to taste with salt and pepper. Tuck the pieces of salt cod among the beans, cover, and cook over very low heat for 10 minutes longer. Serve garnished with chopped parsley and the reserved onion.

MARK BEAN

Elizabeth named this bean for Mark Miller, the chef and creator of Coyote Cafe in Santa Fe, who was her inspiration for getting into agriculture in the first place, and who brought this bean to her from Japan. It's a huge blackish-purple bean, a cousin of the scarlet runner, that keeps its shadowy color after cooking. It has a tantalizingly subtle, smoky flavor that hints of coriander, making it a natural choice for Southwestern dishes, especially those made with cilantro and with chiles that have been roasted and charred. Chipotles and Mark beans are a particularly felicitous combination.

Unsoaked, Mark beans take about 1 1/2 hours to cook.

Substitutes: black runner, chocolate, mauve, Madeira, scarlet runner

Smoky Stewed Mark Beans

Yield: 10 to 12 side dish servings or
6 main course servings

*The hearty, meaty texture of **Mark Miller's** namesake bean makes it excellent for long, slow cooking so it soaks up the flavor of chipotles and fragrant spices like anise, coriander, and pepper. Miller likes to serve this dish with lamb or braised short ribs, especially buffalo short ribs, though it can stand alone for a vegetarian main course. He does not pre-soak the beans because he feels it diminishes their flavor.*

1 pound Mark beans, rinsed

7 quarts water

2 heads garlic, unpeeled
    and sliced in half
    horizontally

1 large onion, peeled and
    quartered

2 large jalapeños, halved

4 large canned or dried chipotles

1/2 teaspoon anise seeds, toasted

1 teaspoon coriander seeds, toasted and ground

1/2 teaspoon dried thyme

1 tablespoon freshly ground black pepper

2 large bay leaves

2 tablespoon salt, or more, to taste

3 large ripe tomatoes, blackened over a flame
and chopped

$^1/_2$ cup chopped cilantro

Grated zest of 1 lemon

3 to 4 tablespoons Tuscan olive oil

Place the beans in a 6 quart pot with the garlic, onion, jalapeños, chipotles, anise seeds, coriander, thyme, pepper, and bay leaves. Add 2 quarts of water, bring to a boil, then reduce heat to a very low simmer. Partly cover the pot and cook about 2 hours. Add another 2 quarts of water, cook another 2 hours. Add another 2 quarts of water.

After the beans have cooked 4 hours and most of the water has been absorbed, add another quart of water along with the salt. Cook just until most of the water has evaporated but the beans are still a bit soupy. Add the tomatoes and cilantro and season with more salt, if necessary. Total cooking time is 5 to 6 hours.

While the beans are cooking, infuse the lemon zest in the olive oil. Serve the beans with the lemon-oil drizzled on top.

MAUVE

Another beauty in the runner family, these giant lavender beans with black specks keep their pretty color after cooking. The beans have a mild baked potato taste.

Unsoaked, mauve beans take about 1½ hours to cook.

Substitutes: black runner, chocolate, Madeira, scarlet runner, white Aztec

Marinated Mauves

These beans are mild enough to need some kind of punchy flavors. A tangy marinade in which the beans are allowed to soak for many hours almost pickles them. The result? A bean nibble, the beans themselves big enough to impale on toothpicks, to serve, like olives, with cocktails; or, like cornichons, alongside a pâté or other charcuterie. Other giant runners can be prepared the same way.

$^{1}/_{4}$ cup mauve beans

3 tablespoons red wine vinegar

2 tablespoons extra virgin olive oil

Salt

Crushed red pepper

1 teaspoon olive paste

1 cup pitted kalamata olives (optional)

Place the beans in a saucepan, cover them with water to a depth of 2 inches, bring to a boil, and simmer, partially covered, for about 1 hour and 15 minutes, or until tender. Drain.

Combine the vinegar and olive oil, and season to taste with salt and crushed red pepper. Stir in the olive paste. Toss the dressing with the beans. Allow to marinate, refrigerated, for at least 24 hours. Fold in the olives, if desired.

Serve as an hors d'oeuvre, with toothpicks.

MAYFLOWER

There is a bit of legend here. This small brownish round bean with white flesh and a deliciously sweet, winey flavor, supposedly came over on the Mayflower. The tale begs credibility. Nonetheless it's a valuable heirloom bean that has more character than some other smallish beans do. It's one of Elizabeth's rarest beans.

Unsoaked, Mayflower beans take about 1 hour to cook.

Substitutes: navy, soldier

Mayflower Beans Baked with Rosemary and Garlic

Yield: 4 servings

I love the idea of using Mayflower beans to make baked beans. But the character of this recipe, perfumed with rosemary and garlic, has more to do with France than New England, where the beans often have a decidedly sweet component. Here the beans are treated almost like flageolets, to spoon onto a plate of roast lamb, as in the Sunday dinner gigot d'agneau, or to serve along with any other roasted or grilled meat.

- 3 tablespoons extra virgin olive oil
- 1 tablespoon finely chopped garlic
- 1 tablespoon fresh rosemary leaves
- 1^1/$_2$ cups dried Mayflower beans
- Approximately 6 cups veal, chicken, or beef stock
- Salt and freshly ground black pepper
- ^{1}/$_4$ cup dry bread crumbs
- ^{1}/$_2$ tablespoon chopped flat-leaf parsley

Preheat the oven to 325°.

Heat 2 tablespoons of the oil in a heavy 2-quart casserole, preferably terra-cotta or enameled cast-iron. Add the garlic and rosemary and sauté briefly. Then stir in the beans.

Add the stock, bring to a simmer, season to taste salt and pepper, then place in the oven.

Cook, uncovered, for about 2^1/$_2$ hours, or until the beans are fairly tender and most of the liquid has been absorbed. Add a little more stock during cooking if necessary.

Sprinkle the bread crumbs on top and drizzle with the remaining oil. Cook for about 30 minutes longer. Sprinkle with parsley before serving.

NAVY

Like Great Northern beans, navy beans, a member of the common bean family, are ubiquitous. Their name comes from their frequent appearance in the mess halls of the United States Navy. They are also the beans used to make the famous United States Senate bean soup, a traditional, but fairly ordinary, recipe seasoned, ever so slightly, with ground cloves.

Ivory-white navy beans are smaller than Great Northerns. They have a baked potato-like flavor.

Soaked, they take about $1^1/_2$ hours to cook.

Substitutes: Great Northern

Mixed Baked Beans

Yield: 4 to 6 servings

Classic Boston baked beans are made with navy beans. This recipe, adapted from one created by **Lydia Shire** *and* **Susan Regis** *at Biba in Boston, ratchets up the flavor of the dish with the addition of cumin seeds, a jalapeño pepper, and a whiff of orange.*

1 cup dried navy beans

$^1/_2$ cup dried kidney beans

$^1/_2$ cup dried pinto beans

2 sprigs thyme

1 tablespoon cumin seeds

1 tablespoon extra virgin olive oil

1 large onion, chopped

1 carrot, peeled and chopped

$^1/_2$ pound thick-sliced smoked bacon, diced

1 jalapeño chile, seeded and chopped

2 cloves garlic, chopped

$^1/_2$ cup crushed canned tomatoes

4 ripe plum tomatoes, diced

$^1/_4$ cup pure maple syrup

$^1/_4$ cup firmly packed brown sugar

1 bay leaf

Grated zest of 1 orange

$^1/_2$ tablespoon crushed black peppercorns

$^1/_3$ cup chopped fresh cilantro

Approximately ¼ cup cider vinegar
Salt

Place all the beans in a bowl, cover them with cold water to a depth of 2 inches, add the thyme, and allow them to soak for at least 4 hours or overnight.

Heat a heavy 2- to 3-quart casserole. Add the cumin seeds and stir until they begin to dance around and smell toasty. Remove the seeds and set them aside.

Add the oil to the casserole. Sauté the onion, carrot, and bacon for 10 minutes, or until the bacon is golden. Add the jalapeño, garlic, and toasted cumin seeds and cook for a few minutes.

Preheat the oven to 300°.

Drain the beans and add them to the casserole along with the canned and fresh tomatoes, maple syrup, brown sugar, bay leaf, orange zest, and peppercorns. Stir in all but 1 tablespoon of the cilantro.

Add 2 cups of cold water, cover, and bring to a slow simmer. Place the casserole in the oven and cook for 1 hour. Add the vinegar and season to taste with salt. Cook for 1 hour longer, or until the liquid has been absorbed but the beans are still very moist.

Adjust seasonings, adding salt and pepper and up to 2 tablespoons more cider vinegar to taste. Serve, garnished with the remaining cilantro.

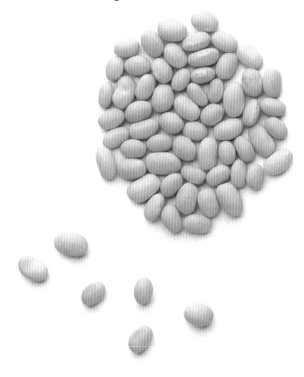

PAINTED PONY

It should come as no surprise that the painted pony is related to the Appaloosa and the pinto. All named for horses, these beans, of Mexican origin, share a slender oval shape and coloration that suggests equine markings. Painted ponys are shaded from beige to black, and though the pattern softens after cooking, the color is retained. They have a rich, nutty flavor.

Unsoaked, painted pony beans take about $1^1/_2$ hours to cook.

Substitutes: Appaloosa, Jacob's cattle, pinto, rattlesnake

Painted Pony, Wild Rice, and Corn Salad

Yield: 8 servings

Here is a variation on rice and beans. Wild rice—not actually a rice, but a grass—is combined with corn and deeply flavorful painted pony beans for a salad that certainly owes a great deal to Native American ingredients. The salad can be prepared up to a day in advance and allowed to marinate.

$^3/_4$ cup painted pony beans

1 cup raw wild rice

1 cup cooked corn kernels, preferably fresh

1 cup finely chopped, peeled, and seeded ripe
   tomato

$^1/_2$ jalapeño chile, seeded and minced

3 scallions, chopped

3 tablespoons honey mustard

$^1/_2$ cup cider vinegar

$^1/_3$ cup extra virgin olive oil

Salt

1 tablespoon finely minced fresh chives

Place the beans in a saucepan with water to cover to a depth of 2 inches. Bring to a boil and simmer, partially covered, until the beans are tender, about 1 hour if they have been soaked, about $1^1/_2$ hours if they have not been soaked. Be sure the beans are covered with water at all times.

While the beans are cooking, place the wild rice in another saucepan, add 3 cups of water, and bring to a boil. Lower the heat and simmer gently for 45 minutes. Cover the pan and set it aside for 10 minutes.

Transfer the rice to a mixing bowl. Add the corn, tomato, jalapeño, and scallions. When the beans are done, drain and add them to the bowl.

Whisk together the honey mustard and vinegar, then whisk in the olive oil. Fold into the rice and bean mixture. Season to taste with salt. Allow the salad to marinate at room temperature for at least 1 hour. Fold in the chives and serve.

PINTO

Pinto beans, which can be interchanged with cranberry (or Italian borlotti) beans, provide ample evidence of the variety in the kidney bean family. Pintos themselves, which originated in Mexico and South America, come in an array of sizes, with markings of varying intensity.

The best pintos are fairly large, plump, pinkish-brown ovals that have a mildly nutty taste. They are widely sold in supermarkets.

Unsoaked, pinto beans take about 2 hours to cook.

Substitutes: cranberry, Appaloosa, kidney, painted pony, rattlesnake

Sherried Pinto Bean Soup

Yield: 4 servings

This is a beautifully mellow soup, a bit milder than a typical black bean soup, which it resembles. The ginger combined with the chile gives it a pleasant bit of heat.

- 1 cup dried pinto or cranberry beans, soaked if desired
- 2 tablespoons extra virgin olive oil
- 1 tablespoon peeled minced fresh ginger
- $1/2$ jalapeño chile, seeded and minced
- 1 red bell pepper, seeded, veins removed, and minced
- 1 medium onion, chopped
- 1 tablespoon oloroso sherry
- Salt and freshly ground black pepper to taste
- $1/3$ cup sour cream, crème fraîche, or whole-milk plain yogurt

Place the beans in a saucepan, cover with 6 cups cold water, and bring to a boil. Reduce the heat and simmer, partially covered, until the beans are very tender, about 1 hour if they have been soaked, $1^1/2$ hours unsoaked. Drain the beans, reserving the cooking liquid.

Heat the oil in a heavy saucepan. Add the ginger, jalapeño, bell pepper, and onion and sauté until tender. Stir in the beans. Transfer to a food processor or blender and purée, adding most of the bean cooking liquid, to make a smooth soup that is about the consistency of a cream sauce. It should not be too thick.

Transfer the soup to a saucepan and bring to simmer. Stir in the sherry. Season to taste with salt and pepper. Serve with a dollop of sour cream, crème fraîche, or yogurt.

RAQUEL

The Raquel is one of Elizabeth's favorite beans. And it's easy to understand why. Not only does she believe she has traced its origins to the Chihuahua region in the Sierra Madre of northern Mexico, but this desert, or tepary, bean has a seductively toasty flavor.

It's a medium-small oval, prettily patterned in butterscotch and white. After cooking the white turns beige.

Unsoaked, Raquel beans take 1 1/2 hours to cook.

Substitutes: Jacob's cattle, Mayflower, painted pony, Steuben yellow eye

Warm Raquel Bean Salad

Yield: 6 to 8 servings

This is one of the simplest of bean salads, Italian in its inspiration. Serve it warm or at room temperature. If Raquel beans are not available, there are many possible substitutes, including not only the ones mentioned above, but also some more commonplace beans, like cranberry, cannellini, flageolet, Great Northern, navy, and pinto.

$1^{1}/_{2}$ cups dried Raquel beans, soaked if desired

2 teaspoons finely chopped garlic

4 medium ripe tomatoes, peeled, seeded, and chopped

2 ounces prosciutto, in 1 piece

2 sprigs rosemary

$^{1}/_{4}$ cup chopped flat-leaf parsley

$^{1}/_{3}$ cup extra virgin olive oil

Juice of 1 lemon

Salt and freshly ground black pepper to taste

Drain the beans and place them in a saucepan with water to cover to a depth of 2 inches. Bring to a simmer and cook, partially covered, until they are tender but still hold their shape, 45 minutes to 1 hour 15 minutes. Allow them to cool in their cooking liquid until they are just warm. Drain well and place in a mixing bowl.

Gently fold in the garlic and tomatoes. Dice the prosciutto and strip the rosemary leaves from the stems and add these ingredients along with the parsley and all but 2 tablespoons of the olive oil to the beans. Fold in gently. Fold in the lemon juice and season to taste with salt and pepper.

Transfer to a serving dish and drizzle with the remaining oil, then serve while still warm.

RATTLESNAKE

These slender oval, brown speckled beans, a new hybrid that has a slightly more intense flavor than the pintos to which they are related, turn brown and plump once cooked. They have a seductively rich, winey flavor, making them excellent stewed, in soups and casseroles, and as a side dish.

Unsoaked, rattlesnake beans take 1^1/$_2$ hours to cook.

Substitutes: pinto, soldier, Swedish brown

Sea Scallops with Rattlesnake Beans and Thyme

Yield: 4 servings

Jimmy Schmidt, *the chef and co-owner of the Rattlesnake Club in Detroit, has long been devoted to Elizabeth's beans. Originally, this recipe called for shrimp, making it similar to the Warm Shrimp and Cannellini Salad (see page 43) that so many chefs have adapted from San Domenico. But it is excellent with scallops. And instead of cannellini, it's only appropriate that rattlesnake beans be used. They provide more assertive flavor, which the lush scallops can handle easily.*

^{1}/$_2$ cup dried rattlesnake beans, soaked if
    desired

1 medium onion

1 bunch fresh thyme, stems and leaves
    separated

2 tablespoons extra virgin olive oil

1 pound sea scallops

1 clove garlic, minced

6 large ripe tomatoes, peeled, seeded, very finely
    diced and drained

^{1}/$_2$ cup dry white wine

^{1}/$_2$ cup fish stock or water

2 tablespoons balsamic vinegar

Salt and freshly ground black pepper

2 tablespoons snipped fresh chives

Combine the beans and onion in a large pot. Tie the thyme stems together and add them. Cover with cold water to a depth of 2 inches, bring to a simmer, reduce the heat to very low, and simmer, partially covered, for about 2 hours, until the beans are tender. Skim any foam from the surface during cooking.

Remove the onion and thyme stems and drain the beans.

Heat the olive oil in a large heavy skillet over high heat. Pat the scallops dry and add them. Cook until seared, turning them once, about 2 minutes on each side. Remove the scallops from the pan. Add the garlic, tomato, wine, and stock and cook until the liquid has thickened, about 10 minutes.

Add the beans and vinegar, season to taste with salt and pepper, then add half the chives and thyme leaves. Return the scallops to the pan, just long enough to reheat them.

Divide the beans among four warm plates, top each portion with some of the scallops, and sprinkle with the remaining chives and thyme. Serve immediately.

RICE BEAN, WILD RICE BEAN

These are among the tiniest of beans, dwarf versions of the cannellini and other common beans. The tiny white ovals have a mild flavor. They're convenient to keep on hand because, like lentils and adzukis, they cook quickly without soaking. And their blandness makes them good in forcefully seasoned dishes. A related variety is the ebony-colored wild rice bean.

Unsoaked, rice beans take about 1 hour to cook.

Substitutes: wild rice beans

Hacked Chicken with Rice Beans

Yield: 4 servings

This recipe, Chinese in inspiration, is usually made with noodles. But the addition of rice beans makes it a first-rate salad.

1 cup dried rice beans

8 ounces boneless skinless chicken breast

Pinch of salt and freshly ground black pepper

$1^1/_2$ tablespoons creamy unsalted peanut butter

3 tablespoons hot brewed black tea

1 tablespoon light (thin) Chinese soy sauce

1 tablespoon unseasoned rice vinegar

1 teaspoon peeled, minced fresh ginger

$^1/_2$ cucumber, peeled, seeded, and chopped

2 tablespoons chopped scallions

$^1/_2$ teaspoon Chinese chile oil, or to taste

1 tablespoon finely chopped cilantro leaves

Place the beans in a saucepan, cover them with water to a depth of 2 inches, bring to a simmer, and cook gently, partially covered, until the beans are tender, about 1 hour.

Meanwhile, place the chicken in a saucepan, cover it with water, season with salt and pepper, and poach gently for about 30 minutes, until the chicken is cooked through. Drain the chicken and allow it to cool.

Place the peanut butter in a large mixing bowl and dilute it with the tea, mixing until it is smooth. Stir in the soy sauce, vinegar, and ginger. Set aside until the beans are cooked.

Drain the beans and rinse them in cold water. Fold them into the peanut butter mixture. Tear the chicken by hand into small shreds and add it to the bowl along with the cucumber and scallions. Mix all the ingredients together gently, then season with the chile oil.

Transfer the salad to a serving bowl and sprinkle the cilantro over the top. Serve at room temperature.

SCARLET RUNNER

Scarlet runners may be the most common and popular of the runner beans. They are large, flat, mottled mahogany beans that grow in streaky pods on plants known for their spectacular flowers. The nectar of the flowers attracts hummingbirds. The runner bean family is called *Phaseolus coccineus,* derived from cochineal, a red dye and a reference to the bright color of the flowers. These are beautiful beans which originally came from Mexico and were used ceremonially by various Native American civilizations.

The lightly fruity flavor of scarlet runners makes them superb in an array of dishes, most notably salads. Their texture is fairly crisp, enhancing their appeal in salads. Personally, I think the black runner (see page 38) and chocolate (see page 48) varieties are even better, but I'd be happy with scarlet runners any day.

It is best to soak scarlet runners before cooking; unsoaked, they take about $1^1/2$ hours to cook.

Substitutes: black runner, chocolate

Marinated Scarlet Runner Bean Salad

Yield: 6 to 8 servings

This recipe, from **Stephan Pyles,** *the co-owner and chef of Star Canyon in Dallas, is a bean salad and then some. It has a decidedly Tex-Mex personality, but its toothsome intensity makes it perfect for a summer buffet anywhere.*

$2^1/4$ cups dried scarlet runner beans, soaked and
    drained

8 cups vegetable stock or water

1 large yellow onion, peeled and sliced paper
    thin

$^2/3$ cup sherry wine vinegar

2 teaspoons sugar

$^1/2$ teaspoon salt, or to taste

1 red bell pepper, roasted, peeled, seeded, and
    diced

1 yellow bell pepper, roasted, peeled, seeded,
   and diced
1 large ripe tomato, peeled, seeded, and
   chopped
$1/2$ cup pitted oil-cured black olives
3 tablespoons chopped cilantro leaves
1 tablespoon chopped fresh basil
1 cup extra virgin olive oil
2 teaspoons honey mustard
$1/2$ teaspoon ground cumin
1 teaspoon minced garlic
Freshly ground black pepper to taste
8 cups loosely packed assorted young lettuce
   leaves, rinsed and dried.

Place the drained beans in a saucepan and add the broth.
Bring to a boil, reduce the heat, and allow the beans to
simmer, partly covered, until tender, about 1 hour. Drain
and refrigerate the beans.

In a separate bowl, toss the onion with $1/4$ cup of
the vinegar, the sugar and $1/2$ teaspoon salt. Set aside.

When the beans are chilled,
fold in the red and
yellow
bell
peppers, the
tomato, olives,
cilantro, and basil.

Mix the remaining vine-
gar with the olive oil, mustard,
cumin, garlic, salt, and pepper. Fold
$1/2$ cup of this dressing in with the
beans.

In a separate bowl, toss the lettuce
with the remaining vinaigrette dressing.
Arrange the lettuce leaves around the edge of
a large platter and mound the bean salad in
the middle. Garnish with the marinated
onions and serve.

SOLDIER

The distinctive red-brown marking on this common white bean resembles a soldier in Napoleon's army, hence the name. These medium-small oval beans, which, until recently, were more widely available in Europe than in the United States, plump up considerably after cooking. They have a nice fruity flavor and a slightly mealy texture. They would be good in a soup or as a purée, but it is nice to preserve their pattern by cooking them whole.

Unsoaked, soldier beans take 1 hour and 15 minutes to cook.

Substitutes: calypso, Steuben yellow eye

Soldier Beans with Bacon and Cream

Yield: 4 servings

Here are beans at their most seductive, in a rich cream sauce perfumed with sage and bacon. Other smallish but pretty beans like calypsos or Steuben yellow eyes can be used instead of soldiers.

    1 cup dried soldier beans
    2 sprigs sage
    2 ounces pancetta, finely diced
    $^1/_4$ cup chopped shallots
    $^1/_2$ cup heavy whipping cream
    Salt and freshly ground black pepper

Place the beans and sage in a heavy saucepan, cover them with water to a depth of 2 inches and bring to a boil. Lower the heat and simmer gently until the beans are just tender, about $1^1/_2$ hours. Drain the beans.

Place the pancetta in a large preferably nonstick skillet and cook over medium heat until it is lightly browned. Add the shallots and continue cooking until the shallots are golden, about 7 minutes. Stir in the cream and bring to a boil, then lower the heat and fold in the drained beans.

Continue cooking over low heat, stirring, for about 10 minutes longer, or until the cream has thickened enough to cling to the beans. Season to taste with salt and pepper and serve.

SOYBEANS

Soybeans are the bread and butter of China, and also of Japan, more appreciated in every possible form—from sprouts to cooking residue—than as whole beans. Soy sauce, tofu, miso, soybean milk, fermented black beans, tempeh, oil, flour, and bean sprouts are just some of the soybean's various guises. No wonder the Japanese call them *daizu,* meaning "great bean." The protein content of the soybean is higher than that of any other bean. It is the world's most widely consumed bean, and not just by humans.

Soybeans are important as livestock feed in the United States, where they are also turned into plastics, all kinds of imitation foods (soy protein, as in the vegetable "bacon" on the salad bar, for example), and adhesives. You'll see soybean futures traded on commodoties markets around the world.

The soybean may be least appreciated as a whole bean. Unsoaked, soybeans take at least 3 hours to cook.

Substitutes: none

Soybeans with Chanterelles and Spinach

Yield: 4 servings

I soaked and cooked some soybeans and discovered that their uniquely firm texture made it possible to sauté them until they began to brown and turn nutty. Many people find the flavor too aggressive. Try them in this delicious preparation and you may disagree.

1 cup dried soybeans

$^1/_4$ cup extra virgin olive oil

1 onion, finely chopped

2 scallions, finely chopped

4 large cloves garlic, sliced thin

6 ounces fresh small chanterelles (the smaller the better)

$^1/_4$ cup dried currants

Salt and freshly ground black pepper

2 cups rinsed, coarsely chopped fresh spinach, heavy stems removed

$1^1/_2$ tablespoons sherry wine vinegar

Rinse the soybeans in cold water, then place them in a bowl. Cover them with water to a depth of 2 inches and allow them to soak for at least 4 hours.

Rinse the soybeans well, place them in a heavy saucepan, cover them with fresh water to a depth of 3 inches, bring to a simmer, and cook, partially covered, until the beans are tender, about 3 hours. Skim any foam from the surface during cooking. Drain the soybeans.

Heat the olive oil in a large, heavy skillet. Add the onion, scallions, and garlic and sauté until they soften. Add the soybeans and chanterelles and sauté over medium-high heat until the soybeans just start to brown. Add the currants and season to taste with salt and pepper.

Add the spinach, stir-fry until it just wilts, then stir in the vinegar. Remove from the heat, adjust seasonings, and serve immediately.

SPLIT PEAS

As their name implies, split peas, which come in green and yellow varieties, are dried peas that have been peeled and split, so they cook faster. They do not retain their shape after cooking, which makes them excellent candidates for purées.

Peas probably originated in Asia, in northern India or Burma, and may be the oldest of all legumes. Remnants in one cave have been carbon-dated to nearly 12,000 years ago. Peas, which flourish in relatively cool climates, have been found in Stone Age, Iron Age, and Bronze Age sites throughout Europe.

Peas were grown in ancient Greece and Rome, and until the Renaissance, when Italians began developing *piselli novelli* to eat fresh, peas were always dried.

Recipes for dried peas, usually soups, are common in English, Dutch, and Scandinavian cooking. Think of "pease porridge hot..." In Sweden, *arter med flask* is the traditional Thursday supper dish, a thick yellow split pea soup, commemorating King Eric XIV, an unpopular monarch whose last meal was yellow pea soup poisoned with arsenic.

The early Spanish, French, and English settlers of the New World brought dried peas and began harvesting them by the sixteenth century. But it was not until the late nineteenth century that split peas, the dried peas with their indigestible skins rubbed off, began to be produced. Today Canada has become the largest source for split peas in the world.

Unsoaked, split peas take about 1 hour to cook.

Substitutes: lentils

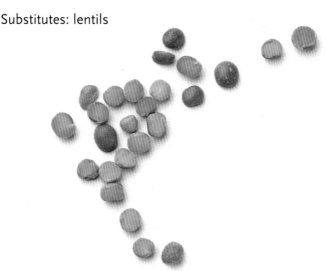

Curried Yellow Split Pea Soup

Yield: 6 servings

The color of yellow split peas is intensified by using curry seasonings.

3 tablespoons vegetable oil

2 onions, chopped

2 Granny Smith apples, peeled, cored, and chopped

2 cloves garlic, minced

1 tablespoon peeled minced fresh ginger

1 tablespoon curry powder

1 tablespoon ground cumin

1 teaspoon ground mustard

1 pound yellow split peas

Salt and freshly ground black pepper

Juice of 1 lime

1 tablespoon finely chopped cilantro leaves

1/3 cup plain yogurt

Heat the oil in a large, heavy saucepan. Add the onions, apples, garlic, and ginger and sauté over medium-low heat until soft but not brown. Stir in the curry powder, cumin, and mustard.

Stir in the peas, add 7 cups of water, bring to a simmer, cover, and cook very slowly for 1 hour, or until the peas are tender. Add a little more water if needed.

Purée the soup in a food processor or blender, in more than 1 batch if necessary.

Return the soup to the saucepan and bring it to a simmer. Season to taste with salt and pepper. Add more water if the soup is too thick.

Mix the cilantro and yogurt together. Serve the soup with a dollop of the yogurt on top of each portion.

STEUBEN YELLOW EYE

There are a number of medium-size white beans marked with golden to brown splotches, or "eyes." This one, sometimes called the Maine yellow eye, has a mustard-colored spot. Another well-known example of a bean with similar marking is the black-eyed pea. The Steuben yellow eye plumps up nicely and turns ivory-brown after cooking. It has a velvety texture beneath a thin skin and a lovely mellow flavor. It's an excellent bean for salads and stews.

Unsoaked, Steuben yellow eyes take about $1^1/_2$ hours to cook.

Substitutes: calypso, navy, soldier

Steuben Yellow Eye Beans Baked with Pasta, Basil, and Ricotta

Yield: 6 servings

Deborah Madison, *chef and vegetable expert, has been a regular at Elizabeth's bean tastings. Her recipe combines beans with pasta, herbs, and cheese for a substantial main dish. A salad and some crusty bread are the only accompaniments needed.*

1 cup dried Steuben yellow eye beans, soaked

6 tablespoons extra virgin olive oil

$^1/_2$ medium onion, finely chopped

1 bay leaf

6 sprigs thyme, or $^1/_2$ teaspoon dried

Salt

3 large cloves garlic

2 cups loosely packed fresh basil leaves

1 cup freshly grated Parmesan cheese

Freshly ground black pepper

$1^1/_2$ cups dried pasta, in small shapes like shells

2 large ripe tomatoes, peeled, seeded, and chopped

1 cup ricotta cheese

1 cup dry bread crumbs

Place the beans in a saucepan, cover them with water, bring to a boil, and simmer for 10 minutes, then drain.

Heat 1 tablespoon of the oil in a large pot over medium heat. Add the onion, bay leaf, and thyme. Cook for several minutes, then add the beans and 8 cups of water. Simmer, partially covered, until the beans are nearly tender, about 45 minutes. Season with salt and cook for 15 minutes longer. Remove the pot from the heat and set it aside to cool.

Turn on a food processor and drop the garlic cloves in through the feed tube. Then push the basil leaves into the processor and process until minced. Turn off the processor and scrape down the sides of the container. Turn the machine on again and add the Parmesan cheese and all but 1 teaspoon of the remaining oil, gradually. Season the purée to taste with salt and pepper.

Preheat the oven to 350°. Use the remaining oil to grease an 8-cup gratin dish. Bring a large pot of salted water to a boil.

Add the pasta to the boiling water and cook until al dente, about 8 minutes. Drain and rinse the pasta under cold water, then drain again.

Add the pasta to the beans in their broth, along with the tomatoes. Spread the mixture into the baking dish. Nestle clumps of the ricotta cheese and the basil mixture among the other ingredients. Lightly press the bread crumbs over the surface and bake until browned, about 35 minutes.

Serve hot or at room temperature.

SWEDISH BROWN

The one thing you learn about the names of beans is that they are descriptive, not frivolous. These toasty brown, medium-size oval beauties, each with a white spot, were supposedly brought to the United States by Swedish immigrants who settled in Montana in the nineteenth century. They are popular in the northern Midwest because they mature early, making them suitable for colder climates. These beans originated in South America, where they may have been grown in the cooler climates of the higher altitudes.

Swedish brown beans turn a pretty honey brown when cooked and have a rich, slightly sweet flavor.

Unsoaked, they take 1 hour and 45 minutes to cook.

Substitutes: Appaloosa, Jacob's cattle, painted pony, rattlesnake, Steuben yellow eye

Swedish Brown Bean Canapés

Yield: 24 to 30 canapés

Just about any bean can be mashed and used for these canapés, and this recipe is easy to prepare with canned beans. For a crowd, make them with several kinds of canned beans: black, kidney, and cannellini.

24 to 30 thin slices French baguette bread

1 cup cooked, drained Swedish brown beans or
   kidney beans

3 tablespoons freshly squeezed lemon juice

3 tablespoons finely minced oil-packed
   sundried tomatoes

Salt and freshly ground black pepper

2 egg whites

3 tablespoons freshly grated Parmesan cheese

Preheat the broiler. Lightly toast the baguette rounds, then arrange them on an aluminum foil–lined baking sheet.

Purée the beans in a food processor along with the lemon juice and sundried tomatoes. Season to taste with salt and pepper and transfer to a bowl.

Beat the egg whites with a pinch of salt until they hold firm peaks but are still creamy. Stir one fourth of the egg whites into the bean mixture, then fold in the rest.

Spoon some of this mixture onto each of the toasted bread rounds, covering the bread completely. Sprinkle each canapé with a little of the cheese. Place them under the broiler and broil for 1 to 2 minutes or until lightly browned.

Transfer the canapés to a platter or tray and serve.

TARBAIS

A white bean cultivated in southwest France, the Tarbais is a rarity in the United States. It is named for the city of Tarbes and is traditionaly used to make cassoulet. The medium-large bean holds its shape extremely well and has a mild flavor and a deliciously creamy texture.

Unsoaked, Tarbais beans take about 2 hours to cook.

Substitutes: cannellini

Traditional Cassoulet

Yield: 12 servings

Chef **Laurent Manrique,** *a native of Gascony in France, is fussy about his cassoulet. He worked hard to find an importer to bring in the Tarbais beans he prefers for his recipe, made with duck.*

> 4 cups white vinegar
>
> 4 cups Tarbais or cannellini beans
>
> 1/2 cup duck fat
>
> 1 pound slab bacon, diced
>
> 2 pounds garlic sausage, cut into 1-inch slices
>
> 2 large onions, chopped
>
> 8 cloves garlic, minced
>
> 1 pound prosciutto, cubed
>
> 1/2 bunch thyme
>
> Approximately 8 cups duck or chicken stock
>
> 6 pieces duck confit (drumsticks and thighs), halved

Place the beans in a large bowl, add the vinegar and enough water to cover the beans by 2 inches, and allow to soak overnight. Drain the beans.

Heat the duck fat in a large, heavy, cast-iron casserole. Add the bacon. Brown and remove the bacon. Then add the sausage. Lightly brown it, then remove the sausage from the casserole.

Add the onions and garlic and sauté until just starting to brown. Add the prosciutto, thyme, and 8 cups of stock.

Preheat the oven to 250°.

Add the beans to the casserole, bring to a very slow simmer, cover, and place in the oven for 45 minutes. Skim the surface. Add the bacon, sausage, and prosciutto and cook for 45 minutes longer. Remove from the oven, allow to cool to room temperature, then cover and refrigerate overnight.

The next day, preheat the oven to 250°. Gently reheat the casserole on top of the stove, adding more stock or water if necessary so the ingredients are very moist. Tuck the duck confit into the casserole, making sure the legs are completely covered, and bake, covered, for 1 hour. Remove from the oven and set aside. Adjust seasonings, adding salt and freshly ground black pepper to taste.

About 1 hour before serving, preheat the oven to 350°. Transfer the cassoulet to an overproof terra-cotta crock, if one is available; if not, leave it in the cast-iron casserole. Place in the oven and bake for 1 hour. Serve.

WHITE AZTEC

A Native American bean that was cultivated by the Anasazi as well as the Aztecs, the white Aztec is big and rounded. It is similar to the white bean French chefs call *coco*. It has an herbaceous flavor and a slightly crumbly texture. Sometimes it's called a potato bean, an apt description. It is a half-runner, related to the big runner beans.

Unsoaked, white Aztec beans take about 1½ hours to cook.

Substitutes: white emergo

Seared Red Snapper with White Aztec Beans and Chanterelles

Yield: 4 servings

Larry Forgione, *the chef and owner of An American Place in Manhattan, among the first restaurants in the country to celebrate American ingredients, was one of Elizabeth's early fans. This recipe combines lush white Aztecs stewed with peppers and chanterelles as a foil for seared red snapper.*

⅔ cup white Aztec beans, soaked if desired, and drained

4 unskinned red snapper fillets, approximately 1½ pounds

Salt and freshly ground black pepper

1 teaspoon chile powder

2 tablespoons extra virgin olive oil

½ cup finely diced poblano chiles

2 large cloves garlic, finely minced

4 ounces fresh chanterelles, brushed clean and quartered

1 ounce sweet sherry

1 tablespoon chopped rosemary leaves

1 cup seafood stock

2 cups young spinach leaves, rinsed

3 to 4 tablespoons chopped flat-leaf parsley leaves

Place the beans in a saucepan, cover them with water to a depth of 2 inches, and bring to a boil. Lower the heat and simmer, partially covered, for about 1 hour or longer, until the beans are tender. Be sure the beans are covered with water at all times. Drain and set them aside.

Preheat the oven to 400°.

Score the skin of the snapper fillets in a criss-cross pattern every $1/2$ inch or so. Season with salt, pepper, and chile powder.

Heat the oil in a heavy nonstick pan. Add the fish, skin side down, and sear over medium-high heat 2 to 3 minutes, until browned. Transfer the fish to an ovenproof dish, skin side up, place it in the oven, and cook for 5 to 7 minutes, or until done. Remove from the oven.

Add the poblanos and garlic to the nonstick pan used to cook the fish and sauté for about 1 minute. Stir in the chanterelles and sauté for another minute. Add the sherry, drained beans, rosemary, and stock. Cover and allow to simmer for 3 minutes or so. Season to taste with salt and pepper. Fold in the spinach.

Spoon the bean mixture into each of 4 shallow soup plates. Top each with a snapper fillet, skin side up, sprinkle with parsley, and serve.

WHITE EMERGO

These heirloom bush beans of Mexican origin are as handsome as a white bean can be. They're big and white, with a buttery texture and a tangy, slightly fruity flavor that suggests Parmesan cheese.

Unsoaked, white emergo beans take about 1 1/2 hours to cook.

Substitutes: cannellini, white Aztec

White Emergo and Endive Soup

Yield: 6 servings

To intensify the Parmesan flavor that gives these beans such an intriguing character, I suggest dusting each portion of soup with Parmesan cheese. But be sure to use Parmigiano-Reggiano imported from Italy and grate it fresh.

1 cup dried white emergo beans, soaked
    overnight

1 pound endives

Juice of $1/2$ lemon

2 cloves garlic, minced

Approximately $3^1/2$ cups chicken stock

Salt and freshly ground white pepper

3 tablespoons butter or olive oil

1 cup finely diced white bread

$1/4$ cup freshly grated Parmesan cheese

Place the beans in a heavy saucepan, cover them with water to a depth of 2 inches, bring to a simmer, and cook, partially covered, until the beans are tender, about 1 hour. Skim any foam from the surface during cooking.

Meanwhile, wash the endive and trim off the cores. Chop the leaves and put them in a heavy saucepan with the lemon juice. Cover and cook over very low heat until the endive is tender. Stir in the garlic. Add the $3^1/2$ cups of chicken stock and simmer for 15 minutes. Season to taste with salt and pepper. Remove from the heat and set aside until the beans are tender.

Heat the butter or oil in a small skillet. Add the bread and sauté over medium heat, stirring constantly, until it is lightly browned. Remove the bread from the skillet and place it on paper towels to drain.

Drain the beans and add them to the endive mixture. Purée the beans and endive in a food processor, then return them to the saucepan in which the endive was cooked. Simmer for another 5 minutes. Again, season with salt and pepper and adjust the consistency of the soup, adding additional stock or water if necessary.

Serve the soup with a sprinkling of sautéed croutons and a dusting of Parmesan cheese.

Contributing Chefs

Francesco Antonucci, the chef and co-owner of Remi, a Venetian-style restaurant in Manhattan, is a native of Venice, where beans are highly appreciated. He is the coauthor, with Florence Fabricant and Adam Tihany, of *Venetian Taste* (Abbeville Press, 1994).

Bobby Flay is the chef and co-owner of Mesa Grill and Bolo in Manhattan. His lusty, vibrant cooking borrows heavily from Spain and Mexico.

Larry Forgione, the chef and co-owner of An American Place, Larry Forgione's Coach House, and Rose Hill Grill in Manhattan, is one of the pioneers of the new American cooking. He was among the first to recognize the quality of homegrown ingredients and how they could be used to create the new contemporary cuisine. Elizabeth's beans have always been in his pantry.

Sheila Lukins, a renowned cookbook author and a founder of the Silver Palate, has a great talent for translating the best foods of any region into easily accessible recipes. Her most recent book is *U.S.A. Cookbook* (Workman Publishing, 1997).

Deborah Madison, the former chef at Greens in San Francisco, has written a number of vegetarian cookbooks, including *The Vegetarian Way* (1997).

Laurent Manrique, a native of Gascony, the land of cassoulet, has been the chef at Peacock Alley and is now the chef at Campton Place in San Francisco.

Mark Miller, an anthropologist turned chef, was one of the first to encourage Elizabeth Berry to grow beans. His restaurant empire, which now stretches from Santa Fe to Washington, DC, including San Francisco, keeps the beans on the menus.

Bradley Ogden, the chef and co-owner of The Lark Creek Inn in Larkspur, California, specializes in interpreting and modernizing traditional American cooking.

Alfred Portale, the chef and co-owner of Gotham Bar & Grill in Manhattan, is one of a generation of influential chefs specializing in American cooking.

Stephan Pyles, the Dallas-based chef who is the co-owner of Star Canyon and Aquaknox, is one of the chefs who gave Tex-Mex cachet.

Jimmy Schmidt, the chef and co-owner of Rattlesnake Grill, one of Detroit's top restaurants, is another fan of Berry's beans.

Lydia Shire, the chef/owner of Biba and Pignoli in Boston, and **Susan Regis,** the executive chef of the restaurants, have developed a cuisine that is bold, earthy, and imaginative.

Alice Waters, an icon on the American cooking scene, is known for her steadfast support of all that is fresh and fine in food. She showcases her finds at Chez Panisse and Cafe Fanny in Berkeley, California.

Sources for Beans

Dean & DeLuca
560 Broadway, New York, NY 10012; 800-221-7714.
A large assortment of heirloom and common dried beans are sold retail and mail order.

Elizabeth Berry
Gallina Canyon Ranch
P.O. Box 706
Abiquiu, NM 87510
Write to Elizabeth Berry for order forms and bean descriptions.

Phipps Ranch
P.O. Box 349, Pescadero, CA 94060; 800-279-0889.
This family-run ranch sells scores of different kinds of beans, some of which they have developed.

Seed Savers Exchange
3076 North Winn Road
Decorah, IA 52101
This company specializes in seeds for growers, including heirloom beans.

The Bean Bag
P.O. Box 221430
Sacramento, CA 95822
800-845-BEAN
www.beanbag.net
Free, full-color mail order catalog of heirloom beans, rices, and grains.

Beans on the Internet

There are hundreds of websites that deal with beans on the Internet, many of them just descriptive or only offering recipes. Among those that ship dried beans, at least half are bulk dealers that pack in 50 or 100 pound lots. A few websites offer richly varied assortments that go beyond supermarket staples.

Here are some of the better ones:

Earthy Delights, http://www.earthy.com
This company has quite a good array, especially of unusual lentils.

Gallina Canyon Ranch, http://www. market2k.com/beans
Elizabeth Berry's beans can be ordered from this website.

Global Market Place, http://www.globalfoodmarket.com
More than a dozen kinds of beans and lentils are available, including some heirloom varieties.

Hilyard & Hilquist, http://www.thefoodstores.com
A good array of beans, with an emphasis on Southern limas.

Mountain Sunshine Farms,
http://www.mtnsunshine.home.mindspring.com
This company has one of the most extensive inventories, with good descriptions.

Pecos Valley Spice Co., http://www.pecosvalley.com
A small selection of beans grown in New Mexico.

Bibliography

Bayless, Rick with Deann Groen Bayless and Jean Marie Brownson. *Rick Bayless's Mexican Kitchen.* New York: Scribner, 1996.

Chesman, Andrea. *366 Delicious Ways to Cook Rice, Beans and Grains.* New York: Plume, 1998.

Conran, Caroline, Terence Conran and Simon Hopkinson. *The Essential Cookbook.* New York: Stewart Tabori & Chang, 1997.

Cost, Bruce. *Bruce Cost's Asian Ingredients.* New York: William Morrow, 1988.

Fabricant, Florence. *New Home Cooking.* New York: Clarkson N. Potter, 1991.

Fussell, Betty. *I Hear America Cooking.* New York: Viking Penguin, 1986.

Gabaccia, Donna R. *We Are What We Eat.* Cambridge, Mass.: Harvard University Press, 1998.

Heebner, Lesa. *Calypso Bean Soup.* New Orleans: Collins Publishers, 1996.

McGee, Harold. *On Food and Cooking.* New York: Charles Scribner's Sons, 1984.

McNair, James and Andrew Moore. *James McNair's Beans & Grains.* San Francisco: Chronicle Books, 1997.

Miller, Ashley. *The Bean Harvest Cookbook.* Newtown, Conn.:Taunton, 1997.

Miller, Mark and Mark Kiffin. *Coyote's Pantry.* Berkeley, Cal.: Ten Speed Press, 1993.

Report of the Ad Hoc Panel of the Advisory Committee on Technology Innovation, National Research Council. *Lost Crops of the Incas.* Washington, DC: National Academy Press, 1989.

Root, Waverley. *Food.* New York: Simon & Schuster, 1980.

Rosengarten, David with Joel Dean and Giorgio DeLuca. *The Dean & DeLuca Cookbook.* New York: Random House, 1996.

Rozin, Elisabeth. *Blue Corn and Chocolate.* New York: Alfred A. Knopf, 1992.

Sabbam, Odile Redon Françoise and Silvano Serventi. *The Medieval Kitchen.* Chicago: University of Chicago Press, 1998.

Sass, Lorna. *The New Soy Cookbook.* San Francisco: Chronicle Books, 1998.

Stone, Sally and Martin. *The Brilliant Bean.* New York: Bantam Books, 1988.

———*The Instant Bean.* New York: Bantam Books, 1996.

Tannahill, Reay. *Food in History.* New York: Crown Publishers, 1989.

Tihany, Adam, Francesco Antonucci, and Florence Fabricant. *Venetian Taste.* New York: Abbeville Press, 1994.

Toussaint-Samat, Magelonne translated by Anthea Bell. *History of Food.* Blackwood, NJ: Blackwell, 1992.

Trager, James. *The Food Book.* Old Tappan, NJ: Grossman Publishers, 1970.

———*The Food Chronology.* New York: Henry Holt, 1995.

Ward, Susie, Claire Clifton, and Jenny Stacey. *The Gourmet Atlas.* Indianapolis, Ind.: Macmillan USA, 1997.

Weatherford, Jack. *Indian Givers.* New York: Crown Publishers, 1988.

Photo Captions

page v—Andrew Sebastian separating the natural diversity of the fava bean, by Lois Ellen Frank

page viii—Scarlett runner beans, by Charles Mann

page 6—Gallina Canyon Ranch, by Lois Ellen Frank

page 18—Autumn at Elizabeth's ranch, by Lois Ellen Frank

page 21—Elizabeth Berry with guest sorting beans, by Charles Mann

page 22—Jose Duran checking beans after harvest, by Lois Ellen Frank

page 27—Elizabeth Berry with Blanca, by Charles Mann

page 112—Bean tasting at Coyote Cafe, by Charles Mann

page 114—Bean tasting at Andiamo, by Charles Mann

page 120—Beans, by Charles Mann

Index

A

Adzuki beans
    about, 28
    Adzuki and Asparagus
        Salad, 29
American Place, An, 108
Anasazi beans. *See* Appaloosa
    beans
Antonucci, Francesco, 53, 113
Appaloosa beans, 30
    Bowl of Red with Heirloom
        Beans, 30–31
    as a substitute, 64, 84, 86,
        104
Appetizers. *See* also Salads
    Fava Bean Dip, 57
    Marinated Mauves, 79
    Spicy Hummus Quesadilla
        with Jacob's Cattle–
        Poblano Relish, 64–65
    Swedish Brown Bean
        Canapés, 105
Aristophanes, 13
Asparagus Salad, Adzuki and, 29

B

Baby limas. *See* Lima beans
Bacon and pancetta
    Braised Flageolets with
        Smoked Bacon and
        Wilted Kale, 58–59
    Mixed Baked Beans, 82–83
    Soldier Beans with Bacon
        and Cream, 97
    Traditional Cassoulet,
        106–107
Baked beans

Cholent with Pastrami, 61
Mayflower Beans Baked with
    Rosemary and Garlic, 81
Mixed Baked Beans, 82–83
Steuben Yellow Eye Beans
    Baked with Pasta, Basil,
    and Ricotta, 102–103
Traditional Cassoulet,
    106–107
Beano, 27
Beans. *See also individual*
    varieties
    in the Bible, 8, 9, 25
    buying, 23
    cooking, 23–25
    flatulence and, 14, 26–27
    grains and, 8–9
    health and, 25–26
    heirloom, 16–17
    history of, 7–13
    in literature and art, 13–15
    in myth and magic, 13–15
    soaking, 24, 27
    storing, 23
    today, 15–17
Beef
    Cholent with Pastrami, 61
    Penne with Kidney Bean
        Ragù, 66–67
Beluga lentils, 72
    Calamari and Beluga Lentil
        Risotto, 72–73
    as a substitute, 28
Black beans, 34
    Elizabeth's Favorite Black
        Turtle Bean Stew, 35

Black beans, *cont'd*
    as a substitute, 42
Black-eyed peas
    about, 36
    Hoppin' John, 37
Black runner beans, 38
    Kale, Potato, and Sausage
        Soup with Black Runner
        Beans, 38–39
    as a substitute, 48, 76, 78, 94
Borlotti. *See* Cranberry beans
Bowl of Red with Heirloom
    Beans, 30–31
Broad beans. *See* Fava beans

C

Cabeza de Vaca, Alvar Núñez, 10
Calamari and Beluga Lentil
    Risotto, 72–73
Calypso beans, 40
    Corn and Calypso Gratin, 40
    as a substitute, 42, 96, 102
Canapés, Swedish Brown
    Bean, 105
Cannellini, 42
    as a substitute, 38, 40, 52,
        60, 66, 106, 110
    Traditional Cassoulet,
        106–107
    Warm Shrimp and
        Cannellini Salad, 43
Cartier, Jacques, 10
Cassoulet, Traditional, 106–107
Catherine de Médicis, 10
Ceci. *See* Chickpeas
Chanterelles
    Seared Red Snapper with
        White Aztec Beans and
        Chanterelles, 108–109
    Soybeans with Chanterelles
        and Spinach, 99
Charlemagne, 12
Cheese
    Chickpea and Feta Salad with
        Olives, 45
    Spicy Hummus Quesadilla
        with Jacob's Cattle–
        Poblano Relish, 64–65
    Steuben Yellow Eye Beans
        Baked with Pasta, Basil,
        and Ricotta, 102–103

Chez Panisse, 54
Chicken
    Cholent with Pastrami, 61
    Curried Red Lentil and
        Grilled Chicken
        Casserole, 71
    Hacked Chicken with Rice
        Beans, 93
Chickpeas, 44
    Chickpea and Feta
        Salad with Olives, 45
    Dfina (Moroccan Bean Stew),
        46–47
    history of, 8
    Madeira Beans with Salt Cod,
        74–75
    Spicy Hummus Quesadilla
        with Jacob's Cattle–
        Poblano Relish, 64–65
Chiles
    Chocolate Rancheros, 49
    Seared Red Snapper with
        White Aztec Beans and
        Chanterelles, 108–109
    Smoky Stewed Mark Beans,
        76–77
    Spicy Hummus Quesadilla
        with Jacob's Cattle–
        Poblano Relish, 64–65
Chilis
    Bowl of Red with Heirloom
        Beans, 30–31
    Chocolate Rancheros, 49
    Elizabeth's Favorite Black
        Turtle Bean Stew, 35
    Smoky Stewed Mark Beans,
        76–77
Chocolate beans, 48
    Chocolate Rancheros, 49
    as a substitute, 38, 50, 76,
        78, 94
Cholent with Pastrami, 61
Chowders. *See* Soups
Christmas limas. *See* Lima
    beans
Cicero, 12
Columbus, Christopher, 10
Corn
    Corn and Calypso
        Gratin, 40

Painted Pony, Wild Rice,
and Corn Salad, 85
Cortés, Hernando, 10
Coyote Cafe, 19, 49, 76
Cranberry beans, 52
Fresh Shell Bean Gratin,
54–55
Pasta e Fagiole, 53–54
Sherried Pinto Bean Soup, 87
as a substitute, 42, 60, 66,
74, 86
Crop rotation, 12
Curried Red Lentil and Grilled
Chicken Casserole, 71

D

Daniel, 25
De Menil, Christophe, 15
Dfina (Moroccan Bean Stew),
46–47
Dip, Fava Bean, 57
Duck
Lentil Soup with Duck
Sausage and Sherry, 70
Traditional Cassoulet,
106–107

E

Elizabeth's Favorite Black Turtle
Bean Stew, 35
Endive Soup, White Emergo
and, 111
Epazote, 27
Eric XIV (king of Sweden), 100
Ezekiel, 9

F

Fabaria, 14
Fava beans, 13, 56
Fava Bean Dip, 57
Fresh Shell Bean Gratin,
54–55
history of, 8, 12
in myth and traditions,
13, 14
Fennel seeds, 27
Fish
Madeira Beans with Salt Cod,
74–75
Seared Red Snapper with
White Aztec Beans and
Chanterelles, 108–109

Smoked Trout and Baby Lima
Chowder, 33
Flageolets, 58
Braised Flageolets with
Smoked Bacon and
Wilted Kale, 58–59
Fresh Shell Bean Gratin,
54–55
Flatulence, 14, 26–27
Flay, Bobby, 64, 113
Forgione, Larry, 108, 113
Fresh Shell Bean Gratin, 54–55

G

Gallina Canyon Ranch, 19–20,
115, 116
Garbanzo beans. *See* Chickpeas
Gigande beans. *See* Hija beans
Ginger, 27
Gotham Bar & Grill, 69
Great Northern beans, 60
Cholent with Pastrami, 61
as a substitute, 40, 42, 82
Gratins
Corn and Calypso Gratin, 40
Fresh Shell Bean Gratin,
54–55

H

Hacked Chicken with Rice
Beans, 93
Ham and prosciutto
Hoppin' John, 37
Traditional Cassoulet,
106–107
Warm Raquel Bean Salad, 89
Haricot beans, 8, 10–12
Heirloom beans, 16–17. *See also
individual varieties*
Hija beans
about, 62
Turkish Bean Soup with
Lemon, 63
Hoppin' John, 37
Hummus Quesadilla, Spicy,
with Jacob's Cattle–
Poblano Relish, 64–65

J

Jack and the Beanstalk, 13
Jacob, 8
Jacob's cattle beans, 64

Jacob's cattle beans, *cont'd*
  Spicy Hummus Quesadilla
    with Jacob's Cattle–
    Poblano Relish, 64–65
  as a substitute, 30, 84, 88,
    104

K

Kale
  Braised Flageolets with
    Smoked Bacon and
    Wilted Kale, 58–59
  Kale, Potato, and Sausage
    Soup with Black
    Runner Beans, 38–39
Kidney beans, 66. *See also*
    Cannellini
  Bowl of Red with Heirloom
    Beans, 30–31
  Mixed Baked Beans, 82–83
  Penne with Kidney Bean
    Ragù, 66–67
  Swedish Brown Bean
    Canapés, 105
  toxicity of undercooked, 26
  as a substitute, 30, 34, 42,
    52, 60, 86
Kombu, 27
Kyampsia, 14
Kyanites, 14

L

Lamb
  Bowl of Red with Heir-
    loom Beans, 30–31
  Dfina (Moroccan Bean Stew),
    46–47
Lark Creek Inn, 58
Lentils, 68
  beluga, 72
  Calamari and Beluga Lentil
    Risotto, 72–73
  Curried Red Lentil and
    Grilled Chicken
    Casserole, 71
  history of, 8
  Lentil Salad with Lemon
    Vinaigrette, 69
  Lentil Soup with Duck
    Sausage and Sherry, 70
  Le Puy, 28, 68, 69, 72

in myth, 13
  as a substitute, 28, 100
Lima beans
  baby, 32, 33
  Christmas, 50, 51
  Dfina (Moroccan Bean Stew),
    46–47
  history of, 11
  Smoked Trout and Baby
    Lima Chowder, 33
  toxicity of under-cooked,
    11, 26
  Warm Christmas Lima and
    Shiitake Mushroom
    Salad, 51
  as a substitute, 38, 62
Lukins, Sheila, 30, 113

M

Madeira beans, 74
  Madeira Beans with Salt Cod,
    74–75
  as a substitute, 38, 76, 78
Madison, Deborah, 102, 113
Maine yellow eye beans. *See*
    Steuben yellow eye beans
Manrique, Laurent, 106, 113
Marinated Scarlet Runner Bean
    Salad, 94–95
Mark beans, 76
  Smoky Stewed Mark Beans,
    76–77
  as a substitute, 48
Mauve beans, 78
  Marinated Mauves, 79
  as a substitute, 38, 48, 50,
    74, 76
Mayflower beans, 80
  Mayflower Beans
    Baked with Rose-
    mary and Garlic, 81
  as a substitute, 64, 88
Mesa Grill, 64
Miller, Mark, 19, 49, 76, 113
Mixed Baked Beans, 82–83
Moroccan Bean Stew (Dfina),
    46–47
Mushrooms
  Seared Red Snapper with
    White Aztec Beans and
    Chanterelles, 108–109

Soybeans with Chanterelles
and Spinach, 99
Warm Christmas Lima and
Shiitake Mushroom
Salad, 51

N

Navy beans, 82
Mixed Baked Beans, 82–83
as a substitute, 60, 80, 102
Nuñas, 11

O

Ogden, Bradley, 58, 114

P

Painted pony beans, 84
Painted Pony, Wild Rice, and
Corn Salad, 85
as a substitute, 30, 40, 64,
86, 88, 104
Pancetta. *See* Bacon and pancetta
Pasta
Pasta e Fagiole, 53–54
Penne with Kidney Bean
Ragù, 66–67
Steuben Yellow Eye Beans
Baked with Pasta, Basil,
and Ricotta, 102–103
Pastrami, Cholent with, 61
Peas, 100
Curried Yellow Split Pea
Soup, 101
history of, 7
Penne with Kidney Bean
Ragù, 66–67
Peretti, Elsa, 15, 50
Phaseolus acutifolius, 12
Phaseolus coccineus, 12, 94
Phaseolus lunatus, 11
Phaseolus vulgaris, 11, 42
Phipps, Tom, 48
Pinto beans, 86
Mixed Baked Beans, 82–83
Pasta e Fagiole, 53–54
Sherried Pinto Bean Soup, 87
as a substitute, 52, 60, 66,
84, 90
Plato, 14
Pliny the Elder, 13–14
Plutarch, 14
Portale, Alfred, 69, 114

Potato beans. *See* White Aztec
beans
Potatoes
Dfina (Moroccan Bean Stew),
46–47
Kale, Potato, and Sausage
Soup with Black Runner
Beans, 38–39
Smoked Trout and Baby
Lima Chowder, 33
Pressure-cooking, 24–25
Prosciutto. *See* Ham and
prosciutto
Pyles, Stephan, 94, 114
Pythagoras, 13, 14

Q

Quesadilla, Spicy Hummus,
with Jacob's Cattle–
Poblano Relish, 64–65

R

Raquel beans, 88
Warm Raquel Bean Salad, 89
as a substitute, 64
Rattlesnake beans, 90
Sea Scallops with Rattlesnake
Beans and Thyme, 90–91
as a substitute, 30, 64, 84,
86, 104
Rattlesnake Club, 90
Red Snapper, Seared, with
White Aztec Beans and
Chanterelles, 108–109
Regis, Susan, 82, 114
Remi Restaurant, 53
Rice
Bowl of Red with Heirloom
Beans, 30–31
Calamari and Beluga Lentil
Risotto, 72–73
Curried Red Lentil and
Grilled Chicken
Casserole, 71
Hoppin' John, 37
wild, Painted Pony, Wild
Rice, and Corn Salad, 85
Rice beans
about, 92
Hacked Chicken with Rice
Beans, 93

Risotto
  Calamari and Beluga Lentil
    Risotto, 72–73
Roman beans. *See* Cranberry
    beans
Runner beans, 12, 94. *See also*
    individual varieties

S

Salads
  Adzuki and Asparagus
    Salad, 29
  Chickpea and Feta Salad
    with Olives, 45
  Lentil Salad with Lemon
    Vinaigrette, 69
  Marinated Scarlet Runner
    Bean Salad, 94–95
  Painted Pony, Wild Rice,
    and Corn Salad, 85
  Warm Christmas Lima and
    Shiitake Mushroom
    Salad, 51
  Warm Raquel Bean Salad, 89
  Warm Shrimp and
    Cannellini Salad, 43
Salt Cod, Madeira Beans with,
    74–75
San Domenico, 43
Sausage
  Kale, Potato, and Sausage
    Soup with Black
    Runner Beans, 38–39
  Lentil Soup with Duck
    Sausage and Sherry, 70
  Traditional Cassoulet,
    106–107
Scallops, Sea, with Rattlesnake
    Beans and Thyme, 90–91
Scarlet runner beans, 94
  Marinated Scarlet Runner
    Bean Salad, 94–95
  as a substitute, 38, 48, 50,
    74, 76, 78
Schmidt, Jimmy, 90, 114
Seafood
  Calamari and Beluga
    Lentil Risotto, 72–73
  Sea Scallops with Rattlesnake
    Beans and Thyme, 90–91

Warm Shrimp and
    Cannellini Salad, 43
Seared Red Snapper with White
    Aztec Beans and
    Chanterelles, 108–109
Sea Scallops with Rattlesnake
    Beans and Thyme, 90–91
Seed Savers Exchange, 16, 20,
    115
Selu Tyva, 14
Serra, Richard, 15
Shell beans
  Fresh Shell Bean Gratin,
    54–55
Sherried Pinto Bean Soup, 87
Shire, Lydia, 82, 114
Shrimp, Warm, and Cannellini
    Salad, 43
Smoked Trout and Baby Lima
    Chowder, 33
Smoky Stewed Mark Beans,
    76–77
Soldier beans, 96
  Soldier Beans with Bacon
    and Cream, 97
  as a substitute, 40, 80, 90,
    102
Soups
  Curried Yellow Split Pea
    Soup, 101
  Kale, Potato, and Sausage
    Soup with Black Runner
    Beans, 38–39
  Lentil Soup with Duck
    Sausage and Sherry, 70
  Pasta e Fagiole, 53–54
  Sherried Pinto Bean
    Soup, 87
  Smoked Trout and Baby
    Lima Chowder, 33
  Turkish Bean Soup with
    Lemon, 63
  White Emergo and Endive
    Soup, 111
Soybeans, 9–10, 98
  history of, 8
  nutrition of, 26
  Soybeans with Chanterelles
    and Spinach, 99
  as a substitute, 36

Spicy Hummus Quesadilla
        with Jacob's Cattle–
        Poblano Relish, 64–65
Spinach
    Seared Red Snapper with
        White Aztec Beans and
        Chanterelles, 108–109
    Soybeans with Chanterelles
        and Spinach, 99
"Spirit Cave," 7
Squid
    Calamari and Beluga Lentil
        Risotto, 72–73
Star Canyon, 94
Steuben yellow eye beans, 102
    Steuben Yellow Eye Beans
        Baked with Pasta, Basil,
        and Ricotta, 102–103
    as a substitute, 64, 88, 96,
        104
Stews
    Chocolate Rancheros, 49
    Dfina (Moroccan Bean Stew),
        46–47
    Elizabeth's Favorite Black
        Turtle Bean Stew, 35
Swedish brown beans, 104
    as a substitute, 64, 90
    Swedish Brown Bean
        Canapés, 105

T
Tarbais beans, 106
    Traditional Cassoulet,
        106–107
    as a substitute, 42
Tepary beans, 12
"Three Sisters," 9, 14, 32
Tomatoes
    Bowl of Red with Heirloom
        Beans, 30–31
    Chocolate Rancheros, 49

Penne with Kidney Bean
        Ragù, 66–67
Warm Christmas Lima and
        Shiitake Mushroom
        Salad, 51
Traditional Cassoulet, 106–107
Trout, Smoked, and Baby Lima
        Chowder, 33
Turkish Bean Soup with
        Lemon, 63
Turtle beans. See Black beans

V
Vicia faba, 12
Vongerichten, Jean-Georges, 44

W
Warm Christmas Lima and
        Shiitake Mushroom
        Salad, 51
Warm Raquel Bean Salad, 89
Warm Shrimp and Cannellini
        Salad, 43
Waters, Alice, 54, 114
Weyman, Lola, 21
White Aztec beans, 108
    Madeira Beans with Salt Cod,
        74–75
    Seared Red Snapper with
        White Aztec Beans and
        Chanterelles, 108–109
    as a substitute, 42, 48, 78,
        110
White emergo beans, 110
    White Emergo and Endive
        Soup, 111
    as a substitute, 38, 62, 108
White runner beans, 38
Wild rice beans, 20, 92
Wild Rice, Painted Pony, and
        Corn Salad, 85
Wolfert, Paula, 44

The Authors

FLORENCE FABRICANT, a food columnist for the *New York Times* who reports on trends in the food and restaurant scene, has also written three cookbooks: *Pleasures of the Table* (Harry N. Abrams, 1986), *New Home Cooking*

(Clarkson N. Potter, 1991), and *Venetian Taste* (Abbeville Press, 1994).

ELIZABETH BERRY started growing beans, chiles, and other produce on her New Mexico ranch more than fifteen

teen years ago, mainly to supply chefs, and she now specializes in developing bean varieties for commercial production.

The Photographer

Lois Ellen Frank is a Santa Fe based photographer whose main subject has been food and the culinary arts for many years. Her work can be found in cookbooks from some of the most famous chefs in the United States.

Poster by Elizabeth Berry

EGGPLANT

Over 30 beautifully photographed types of eggplant accompanied by brief descriptions.

24 x 36, $15.00

Books by Mark Miller

THE GREAT SALSA BOOK

Featuring 100 widely varied recipes from tomato to tomatillo, chile to corn, garden to ocean.

4 ¹/₂ x 10 ¹/₄ inches, 160 pages
$14.95 paper (Can $23.95)
ISBN 0-89815-517-7

THE GREAT CHILE BOOK

Full-color handbook showcasing 100 chiles. Includes cooking tips and a heat scale.

4 ¹/₂ x 10 ¹/₄ inches, 160 pages
$14.95 paper (Can $23.95)
ISBN 0-89815-428-6

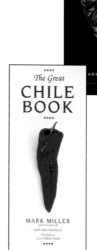

Available from your local bookstore, or by ordering direct from the publisher. Write for our catalogs of over 1,000 books, posters, and tapes.

TEN SPEED PRESS / CELESTIAL ARTS / TRICYCLE PRESS
Box 7123, Berkeley, California 94707
Order phone (800) 841-2665 / Fax (510) 559-1629
order@tenspeed.com • www.tenspeed.com